CORE-PLUS MATHEMATICS PROJECT

Course 1
Part A

Contemporary Mathematics in Context
A Unified Approach

Arthur F. Coxford
James T. Fey
Christian R. Hirsch
Harold L. Schoen
Gail Burrill
Eric W. Hart
Ann E. Watkins
with
Mary Jo Messenger
Beth E. Ritsema
Rebecca K. Walker

Mc Graw Hill Glencoe McGraw-Hill

New York, New York   Columbus, Ohio   Chicago, Illinois   Peoria, Illinois   Woodland Hills, California

Glencoe/McGraw-Hill

A Division of The McGraw·Hill Companies

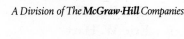

This project was supported, in part, by the National Science Foundation.
The opinions expressed are those of the authors and not necessarily those of the Foundation.

Send all inquires to:
Glencoe/McGraw-Hill
8787 Orion Place
Columbus, OH 43240-4027

ISBN: 0-07-829718-4 (Part A)
ISBN: 0-07-829719-2 (Part B)

3 4 5 6 7 8 9 10 113 10 09 08 07 06 05 04

Contemporary Mathematics in Context
Course 1 Part A Teacher Resources

Contents

Preface

This resource book contains blackline masters prepared to assist you as you teach Course 1, Part A, of the *Contemporary Mathematics in Context* curriculum. As you guide your students though this exciting curriculum, these resources can help you focus student attention on the important mathematics developed in each unit, help your students organize their thinking about specific problems, and save both you and your students valuable preparation time.

In general, three types of masters are included:

■ Masters to help facilitate class discussion

"Think About This Situation" transparency masters

"Checkpoint" transparency masters

Sample responses to open-ended questions

■ Masters to help students organize their responses

Generic plot grids and tables

Generic pages for the students' Math Toolkits, keyed to mathematical themes

Response templates for selected investigations

Unit summary templates

■ Masters to provide additional information or clarification

"Technology Tips" for both TI-82 and TI-83 calculators

Graphs and illustrations from the text, enlarged for easier reading

Graphs and tables supplementing the information in the text

Masters most suited for overhead projector use are labeled "Transparency Master," while those most suited to handouts (or both) are labeled "Activity Master." The *Contemporary Mathematics in Context* Teacher's Guide includes suggested uses for these masters, but it is anticipated that teachers will use these tools in many different ways compatible with their own teaching styles as well.

The most popular activities of teens that go online daily:

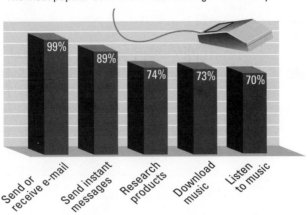

| 99% | 89% | 74% | 73% | 70% |

Send or receive e-mail · Send instant messages · Research products · Download music · Listen to music

Source: Pew Internet and American Life Project

Think About This Situation

As a class, examine the data above from a study of teens who use the Internet. The findings are based on a phone survey of youth ages 12 to 17.

a If a similar study was conducted with online students in your school, do you think the results would be similar? Why or why not?

b Who might find this information important to know? How might they use it?

c The teen interviews were based on a "callback survey" of Internet households identified in a tracking poll as ones in which both the parents or guardians and children had Internet access. Why might the results give an inaccurate picture of the online teen population?

**MASTER
2**

Activity Master

Class Data

Student Name	Height	Armspan	Circumference of Thumb	Circumference of Wrist	Length of Shoe	Length of Stride	One-Minute Pulse Rate Resting	One-Minute Pulse Rate Exercising

Checkpoint

In the three projects, you collected and analyzed measurement data about your group and about your classmates.

a What kinds of relationships did you find in the data from the three projects?

b What pitfalls are possible when you generalize results from a small sample of people, such as your group, to a larger population, such as your class?

c How well did your group cooperate in completing these projects? Write one comment about each group member in the following form.

We appreciated it when . . .

Each person from your group should be prepared to report to the whole class on the group's responses to these questions.

Industry Leaders' Hot Properties

```
1 | 8
2 | 0  1  1  2  7  8
3 | 4  4  7
4 | 5  6  6  9
5 | 0  9
6 | 7
7 | 3
8 |
9 | 0
```

1|8 represents 18.

Describe

4. d. *One possible response*: The artist or group with the largest number of points, 90, was Eminem. This represents an average of only 4 points (a seventh-place vote) from each person. There is a gap from first place to the second place artist, Dr. Dre. The lowest rating is 18 for Britney Spears. Most of the ratings (thirteen) are grouped in the 20s, 30s, and 40s.

**Industry Leaders'
Hot Properties**

**Student Council's
Hot Properties**

1	8
2	0 1 1 2 7 8
3	4 4 7
4	5 6 6 9
5	0 9
6	7
7	3
8	
9	0

1	1 8
2	1 6 8 8 8 9
3	4 6
4	2 3 7
5	4 6 7
6	4 5
7	0 1

1|8 represents 18.

Compare

6. c. *One possible response:* The two distributions are similar in that the top 20 artists were the same for both groups of raters and they gave them about the same total number of points (838 and 828). But the rankings are different. The Student Council's distribution is less spread out than the Industry Leaders' distribution (This is because the new distribution does not have a gap at the high end.) The new distribution is also more evenly spread out, except for the six ratings in the 20s. Another difference is that the lowest rating from the Student Council is 11 which is lower than the lowest rating from the newspaper article. The distributions are similar since they both have the most ratings in the 20s and have half of the ratings below 40.

Checkpoint

In this investigation, you explored characteristics of good written responses.

a What are the important features of a good response when you are asked to *describe* something?

b What are the important features of a good response when you are asked to *explain* your reasoning?

c What are the important features of a good response when you are asked to *compare* two or more things?

Each person from your group should be prepared to share your group's characteristics of good descriptions, explanations, and comparisons.

Checkpoint

Review your work on "Does Education Pay?"

a Compare the information shown in the table and the bar graph. In what ways is the graph better than the table for displaying the data on average monthly earnings? In what ways is it worse?

b How could your analysis of these data be used to plan for your own future?

c How has your group work improved since the first day of class? How could you further improve your group work next time?

Be prepared to share your group's responses with the whole class.

Think About This Situation

Suppose your family wants to buy a used 2001 car that originally sold for between $20,000 and $25,000.

a According to the article, which car did the American Automobile Association (AAA) think was best? Do you think there are any important characteristics that they have omitted?

b There is so much information in the table (on page 15) that it is difficult to see which car might be best. How could you organize or summarize this information to make it more useful in deciding which car to buy?

c Based on the rating table, do you agree with the conclusions drawn by AAA and reported in the article? Why or why not?

Describing Distributions

When describing a distribution, you should discuss each of the following questions.

1. What is the lowest value (the **minimum**)? What is the highest value (the **maximum**)? What items are associated with these values?

2. Are there any **outliers** in the data? That is, are there any values that are unusually large or small and lie out away from the other values? Are there any other unusual values?

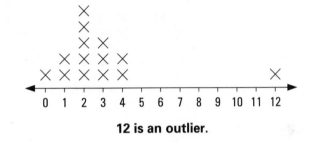

12 is an outlier.

3. Does the plot have one or more peaks?

4. Does the plot appear **symmetric** (the left side looks like a mirror image of the right side)?

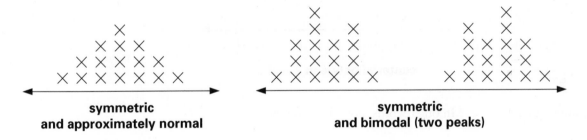

**symmetric
and approximately normal**

**symmetric
and bimodal (two peaks)**

5. If it is not symmetric, does the plot appear to have a tail that stretches to the right? Such a plot is said to be **skewed to the right**. A plot that has a tail that stretches to the left is **skewed to the left**.

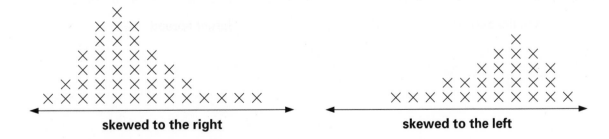

skewed to the right

skewed to the left

Describing Distributions *(continued)*

6. Are there any gaps in the values?

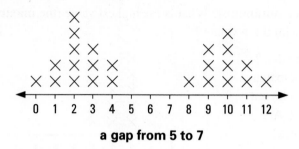

a gap from 5 to 7

7. Where is the distribution centered?

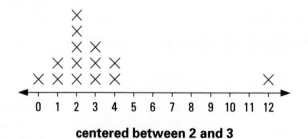

centered between 2 and 3

8. How spread out are the values? In other words, how much do the values vary?

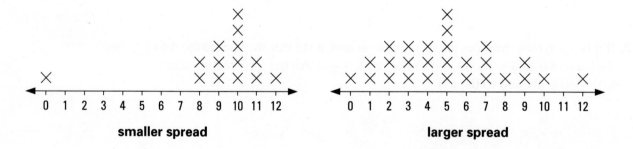

smaller spread   **larger spread**

Checkpoint

You can see important characteristics of a distribution from a histogram or number line plot.

a When would you prefer to make a histogram rather than a number line plot?

b Make a sketch of what you think the histogram of the ages of all women married for the first time last year in the United States might look like. Describe this distribution.

c How might the histogram of the ages of all men married for the first time last year in the United States compare to that of the women?

Be prepared to share your group's thinking and results with the whole class.

Histograms of Car Ratings

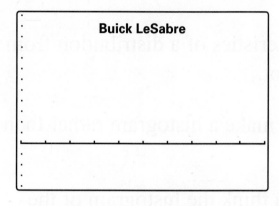

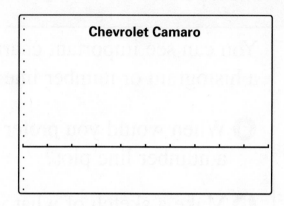

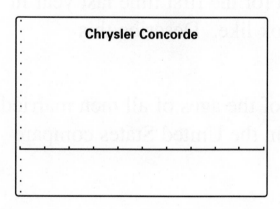

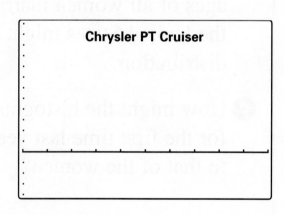

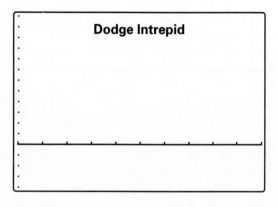

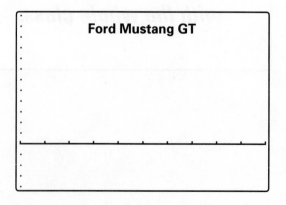

**MASTER
11b**

Histograms of Car Ratings *(continued)*

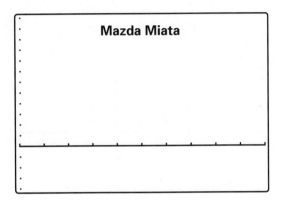

Mazda Miata

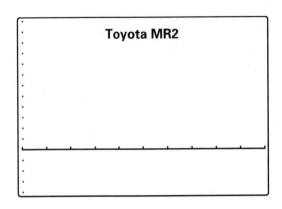

Toyota MR2

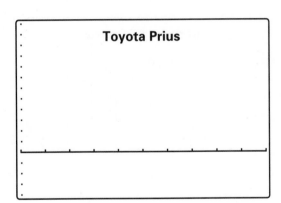

Toyota Prius

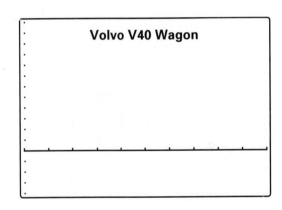

Volvo V40 Wagon

Mazda 626

MASTER
12a

Histogram Key

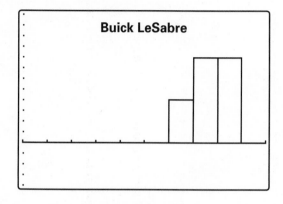

Buick LeSabre

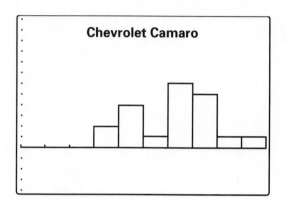

Chevrolet Camaro

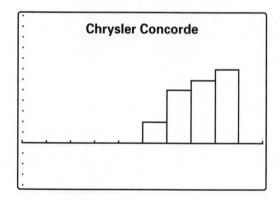

Chrysler Concorde

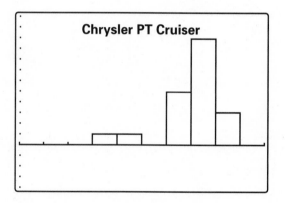

Chrysler PT Cruiser

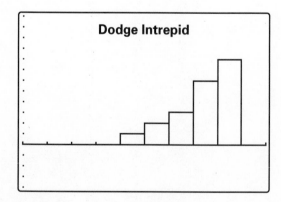

Dodge Intrepid

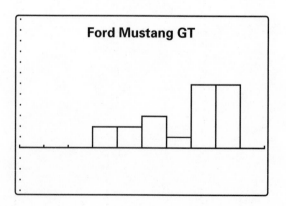

Ford Mustang GT

MASTER
12b

Histogram Key *(continued)*

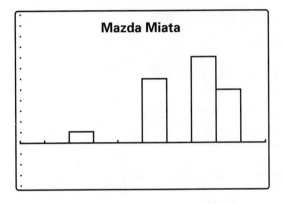

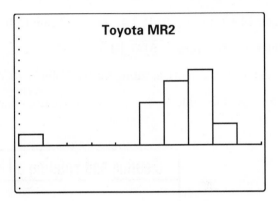

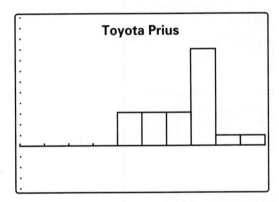

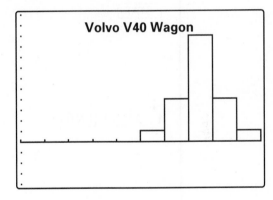

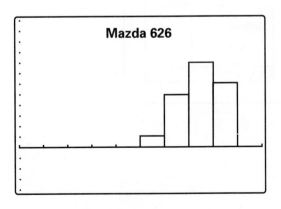

Entering Data in a List

Before entering data into a list, clear the list of previous unwanted entries.

To clear List 1, press [STAT] 4. Then indicate L_1 by pressing [2nd] 1 [ENTER].

To enter the data, press [STAT] 1.

Then enter each numerical rating for the Volvo V40 Wagon followed by [ENTER].

As you type, the value is displayed on the bottom line.

Clearing and Entering a List

Keyboard	Display

[STAT]	```EDIT CALC```
	 ```1:Edit…```
	 ```2:SortA(```
	 ```3:SortD(```
	 ```4:ClrList```

4 [2nd] 1 [ENTER]	```ClrList L1``` ``` Done```

[STAT] 1
 8 [ENTER] 8 [ENTER] 7 *etc.*
	```L1 L2 L3```
	 ```8```
	 ```8```
	 ```—————— ——————```
	
	 ```L1(3)=7```

Displaying a Histogram

To display a histogram of data in a list, you need to specify the viewing window for the graph by selecting values for Xmin, Xmax, Xscl, Ymin, Ymax, and Yscl.

- Xmin is the number where you would like the horizontal axis to begin.
- Xmax is the number where you would like the horizontal axis to end.
- Choosing Xscl = 1 sets the width of each bar of the histogram to be 1.
- Choosing Ymin = –4 leaves room at the bottom of the screen for the text.
- Choosing Ymax = 12 leaves room for a bar 12 units high.
- Selecting Yscl = 1 produces tick marks on the vertical axis that are 1 unit apart.

Press [WINDOW] and use the down arrow ([▼]) key or [ENTER] key to select Xmin.

Because the ratings range from 2 to 10, choose Xmin = 1 and Xmax = 11 by pressing **1** [ENTER] and **11** [ENTER].

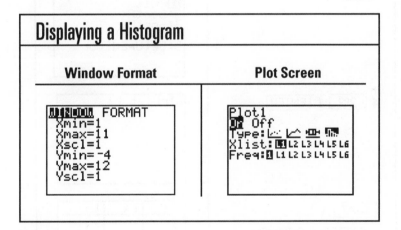

To choose the type of graph, press [2ⁿᵈ] [Y=] **1**. You will see a PLOT SCREEN similar to the one above. Pressing [ENTER] when the cursor is over On turns the plot on. To select the type of plot, arrow down and use the right arrow ([▶]) key to choose the picture of the histogram. Press [ENTER] to finalize your selection. Continue using the arrow and Enter keys to be sure that Xlist selected is L_1 (the data set you want to graph) and the frequency (Freq) is 1.

Now, press [GRAPH] and a histogram for the Volvo V40 Wagon ratings should appear.

Note: If no vertical axis appears on your graph, select FORMAT from the [WINDOW] menu. Then select AxesOn.

MASTER
14a

Entering Data in a List

Before entering data into a list, clear the list of previous unwanted entries.

To clear List 1, press ⌈STAT⌋ **4**. Then indicate L_1 by pressing ⌈2ⁿᵈ⌋ **1** ⌈ENTER⌋.

To enter the data, press ⌈STAT⌋ **1**.

Then enter each numerical rating for the Volvo V40 Wagon followed by ⌈ENTER⌋.

As you type, the value is displayed on the bottom line.

Clearing and Entering a List

Keyboard	Display
⌈STAT⌋	**EDIT** CALC TESTS **1**▪Edit… 2:SortA(3:SortD(4:ClrList 5:SetUpEditor
4 ⌈2ⁿᵈ⌋ **1** ⌈ENTER⌋	ClrList L₁ Done
⌈STAT⌋ **1** **8** ⌈ENTER⌋ **8** ⌈ENTER⌋ **7** *etc.*	L₁ L₂ L₃ 8 ─── ─── ─── L₁(3)=7

Displaying a Histogram

To display a histogram of data in a list, you need to specify the viewing window for the graph by selecting values for Xmin, Xmax, Xscl, Ymin, Ymax, and Yscl.

- Xmin is the number where you would like the horizontal axis to begin.
- Xmax is the number where you would like the horizontal axis to end.
- Choosing Xscl = 1 sets the width of each bar of the histogram to be 1.
- Choosing Ymin = −4 leaves room at the bottom of the screen for the text.
- Choosing Ymax = 12 leaves room for a bar 12 units high.
- Selecting Yscl = 1 produces tick marks on the vertical axis that are 1 unit apart.

Press [WINDOW] and use the down arrow ([▼]) key or [ENTER] key to select Xmin.

Because the ratings range from 2 to 10, choose Xmin = 1 and Xmax = 11 by pressing **1** [ENTER] and **11** [ENTER].

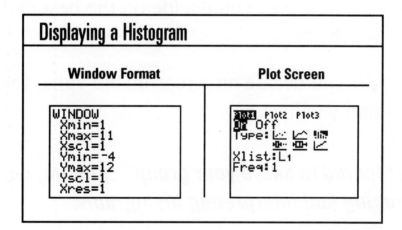

To choose the type of graph, press [2nd] [Y=] **1**. You will see a PLOT SCREEN similar to the one above. Pressing [ENTER] when the cursor is over On turns the plot on. To select the type of plot, arrow down and use the right arrow ([▶]) key to choose the picture of the histogram. Press [ENTER] to finalize your selection. Arrow down to Xlist and press [2nd] **1** to choose L_1 (the data set you want to graph). If needed, arrow down and press [ALPHA] **1** to set the frequency (Freq) to 1.

Now, press [GRAPH] and a histogram of the ratings for the Volvo V40 Wagon should appear in the window.

Note: If no vertical axis appears on your graph, press [2nd] [ZOOM] to get the FORMAT menu. Then select AxesOn.

Checkpoint

In this investigation, you learned how to produce histograms using technology. You also gained more experience in analyzing histograms.

a What does the shape of a distribution tell you about the data?

b If you are producing a histogram with your calculator or computer, how will you decide on the best choice of width for the bars?

c How will you decide on a reasonable value for the maximum *y* value?

Be prepared to share your group's thinking on ways of producing and interpreting histograms.

Think About This Situation

As a class, consider the findings reported on the snacking habits of children and teens.

a The article says that, "Teens have increased their munching from 1 snack a day in 1977 to almost 2."

- Does this mean all teens or a typical teen?

- How could this number have been determined?

b What exactly could the article mean by the statement that "Teens are getting about 610 calories a day from snacks"?

c How could information like this be collected? Which information seems almost impossible to get?

Checkpoint

When displaying and summarizing data, you will need to choose between several possibilities.

a Compare a stem-and-leaf plot to a histogram. How are they alike and how are they different?

b How does a back-to-back stem-and-leaf plot help you compare two distributions?

c Describe three methods of estimating a "typical" value for a distribution.

Compare your thinking and descriptions with those of other groups.

Calculating Measures of Center from Lists

You can use the List operations to calculate measures of center. You must QUIT the List editor (press [2nd] [MODE]) before accessing the List operations.

Press [2nd] [STAT] to access the LIST OPS menu. Use the right arrow ([▶]) key to access the MATH operations for lists.

Accessing List Operations

Keyboard	Display
[2nd] [STAT]	**OPS** MATH 1 SortA(2:SortD(3:dim 4:Fill(5:seq(
[▶]	OPS **MATH** 1 min(2:max(3:mean(4:median(5:sum 6:prod

Note: Be certain to always quit the List editor
([2nd] [MODE]) before accessing the List operations.

For example, you can calculate the mean of data in List 1 from the second display above by choosing option 3 and pressing [2nd] **1** for L_1.

Calculating Measures of Center from Lists

You can use the List operations to calculate measures of center. You must QUIT the List editor (press [2nd] [MODE]) before accessing the List operations.

Press [2nd] [STAT] to access the LIST menu. Use the right arrow ([▶]) key once to access the OPS menu and twice to access the MATH operations for lists.

Accessing List Operations	
Keyboard	**Display**
[2nd] [STAT] [▶]	NAMES **OPS** MATH 1▪SortA(2:SortD(3:dim(4:Fill(5:seq(6:cumSum(7↓ΔList(
[▶]	NAMES OPS **MATH** 1▪min(2:max(3:mean(4:median(5:sum(6:prod(7↓stdDev(

Note: Be certain to always quit the List editor
([2nd] [MODE]) before accessing the List operations.

For example, you can calculate the mean of data in List 1 from the second display above by choosing option 3 and pressing [2nd] 1 for L_1.

Checkpoint

Whether you use the mean, median, or mode depends on why you are computing a measure of center.

a What are the advantages and disadvantages of each measure of center for summarizing a set of data?

b Describe how to find or estimate the mean, median, and mode from a histogram.

Be prepared to share your group's thinking with the whole class.

Heights from Birth to 14

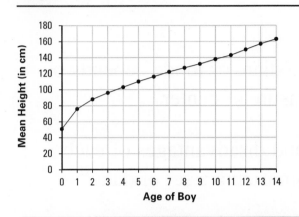

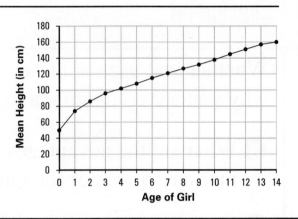

Think About This Situation

The data in the growth charts above come from a physican's handbook. Use the plots to answer the following questions.

a Is it reasonable to call a 14-year-old boy "taller than average" if his height is 165 cm? Is it reasonable to call a 14-year-old boy "tall" if his height is 165 cm? What additional information about 14-year-old boys would you need to know to be able to say that he is "tall"?

b At what height would you be willing to call a 14-year-old girl "tall"? Do you have enough information to make this judgment?

c During which year do children grow most rapidly?

Calculating the Five-Number Summary

You can find the five-number summary on your calculator by selecting 1-Var Stats under CALC in the STAT menu. When the calculator displays 1-Var Stats, enter the name of the list that contains the data. Scroll down the statistics display to see the values of the five-number summary.

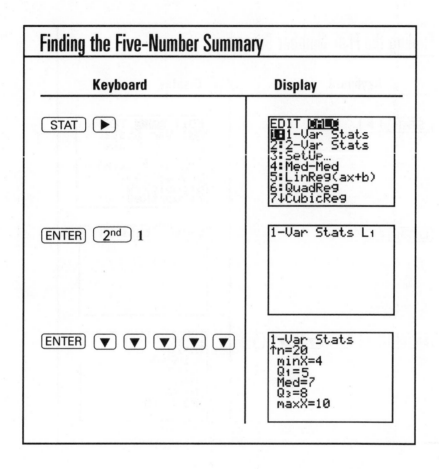

Finding the Five-Number Summary

Keyboard	Display
[STAT] [▶]	EDIT **CALC** **1:** 1-Var Stats 2: 2-Var Stats 3: SetUp... 4: Med-Med 5: LinReg(ax+b) 6: QuadReg 7↓CubicReg
[ENTER] [2nd] 1	1-Var Stats L₁

[ENTER] [▼] [▼] [▼] [▼] [▼]	1-Var Stats
	↑n=20
	  minX=4
	  Q_1=5
	  Med=7
	  Q_3=8
	  maxX=10

Note that if the data for which you want the summary were entered in List 5, the second keyboard line above would be [ENTER] [2nd] **5**.

MASTER
23

Calculating the Five-Number Summary

You can find the five-number summary on your calculator by selecting 1-Var Stats under CALC in the STAT menu. When the calculator displays 1-Var Stats, enter the name of the list that contains the data. Scroll down the statistics display to see the values of the five-number summary.

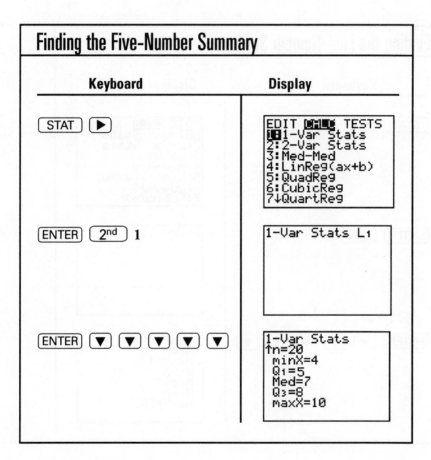

Finding the Five-Number Summary

Keyboard	Display
STAT ▶	EDIT **CALC** TESTS **1** 1-Var Stats 2:2-Var Stats 3:Med-Med 4:LinReg(ax+b) 5:QuadReg 6:CubicReg 7↓QuartReg
ENTER 2nd 1	1-Var Stats L₁

ENTER ▼ ▼ ▼ ▼ ▼	1-Var Stats
	↑n=20
	  minX=4
	  Q₁=5
	  Med=7
	  Q₃=8
	  maxX=10

Note that if the data for which you want the summary were entered in List 5, the second keyboard line above would be ENTER 2nd **5**.

Checkpoint

A percentile gives the location of a value in a set of data while the range and IQR are measures of how spread out the data are.

a Will the range be changed if an outlier is added to a data set? Will the interquartile range be changed?

b Why does the interquartile range tend to be a more useful measure of a data set's variability than the range?

c If you get 75 points out of 100 on your next math test, can you tell what your percentile is? Explain.

d Give an example of when you would want to be in the 10th percentile rather than in the 90th.

e Give an example of when you would want to be in the 90th percentile rather than in the 10th.

Be prepared to share your group's thinking and examples with the rest of the class.

Displaying a Box Plot

To make a box plot of the ratings for the V40 Wagon given on page 50, enter the data in L_1. Next press WINDOW and select Xmin = 1, Xmax = 11, and Xscl = 1. When making a box plot, it is best to select Ymin = 0. You don't need to choose values for Ymax or Yscl. (But be sure Ymax > 0.)

To access the STAT PLOT menu press 2ⁿᵈ Y= . Plot 1 is already highlighted so to select it, press ENTER . Use the down arrow key to select Type. Use the right arrow and Enter keys to select the box plot (see below). Be sure the Xlist selected is L_1 and the Frequency is 1. Now the settings are ready. Press GRAPH to display the plot. A box plot of the ratings for the V40 Wagon should be on the display.

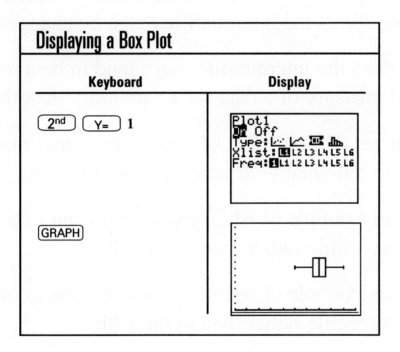

If you press TRACE , the cursor will appear at the median with the value and label in the bottom left of the screen. The right and left arrow keys will move the cursor to the quartiles and the extreme values.

Displaying a Box Plot

To make a box plot of the ratings for the V40 Wagon given on page 50, enter the data in L_1. Next press $\boxed{\text{WINDOW}}$ and select Xmin = 1, Xmax = 11, and Xscl = 1. When making a box plot, it is best to select Ymin = 0. You don't need to choose values for Ymax or Yscl. (But be sure Ymax > 0.)

To access the STAT PLOT menu press $\boxed{\text{2nd}}$ $\boxed{\text{Y=}}$. Plot 1 is already highlighted so to select it, press $\boxed{\text{ENTER}}$. Use the down arrow key to select Type. Use the right arrow and Enter keys to select the box plot (see below). Be sure the Xlist selected is L_1 and the Frequency is 1. Now the settings are ready. Press $\boxed{\text{GRAPH}}$ to display the plot. A box plot of the ratings for the V40 Wagon should be on the display.

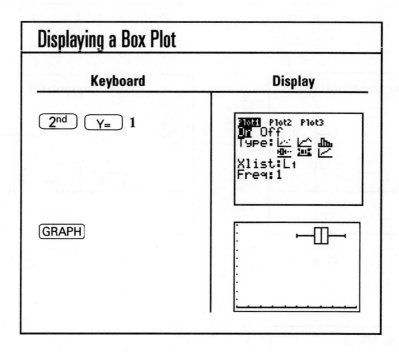

If you press $\boxed{\text{TRACE}}$, the cursor will appear at the median with the value and label in the bottom left of the screen. The right and left arrow keys will move the cursor to the quartiles and the extreme values.

Histograms

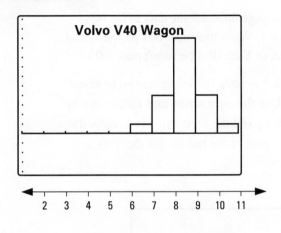

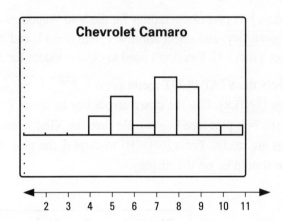

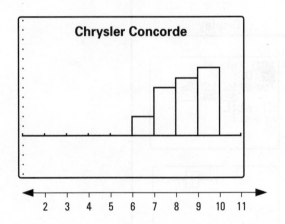

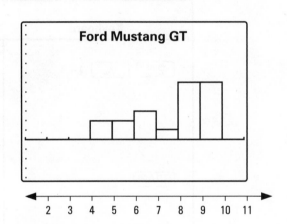

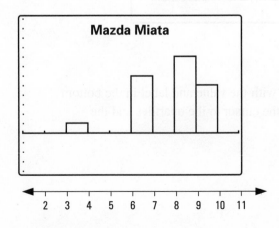

Histograms and Box Plots

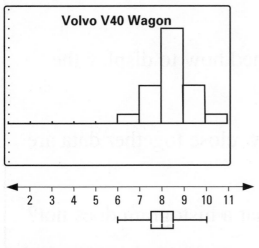

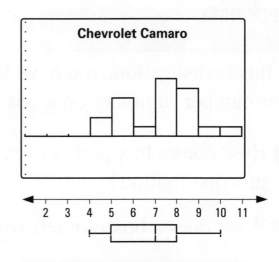

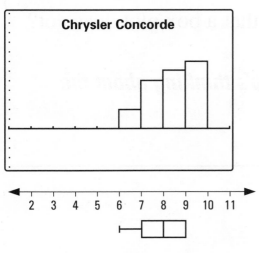

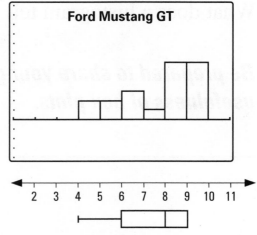

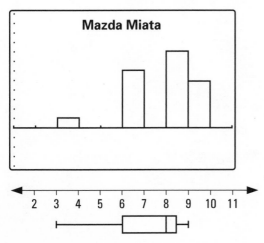

Checkpoint

In this investigation, you have learned how to display the five-number summary on a box plot.

a How does a box plot convey how close together data are in a distribution?

b What does a box plot tell you that a histogram does not?

c What does a histogram tell you that a box plot does not?

Be prepared to share your group's thinking about the usefulness of box plots.

Checkpoint

In this investigation, you learned about the MAD—a measure of variation about the mean of a distribution.

a Why is it important to measure variability?

b Describe two ways of measuring and reporting variability in a data set.

c Which would you expect to have a smaller mean absolute deviation, the distribution of current prices of blue jeans or the distribution of current prices of new compact discs? Explain your reasoning.

Be prepared to share your group's descriptions and thinking with the entire class.

Calculating the MAD

Shown below is a procedure for calculating the mean absolute deviation on a TI-82 calculator. Follow this procedure using the sample data: 7, 3, 2, 5, 6, and 4.

1. First clear List 1 and enter the data into List 1.

2. Find the mean of the data in List 1 using 1-Var Stats from the STAT/CALC menu. The mean is $\bar{x}$.

3. To place the distance of each data value from the mean in List 2, first view the lists and then place the cursor on top of L_2.

4. Because the mean is 4.5, press [2nd] [x⁻¹] [(] [2nd] 1 – 4.5 [)] [ENTER]. The command abs(L_1 – 4.5) removes any negative signs from the differences before they are stored in L_2; "abs" stands for absolute value.

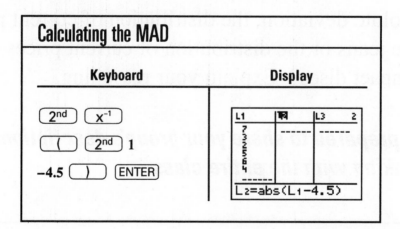

5. Use 1-Var Stats to get the average of L_2. This average is the mean absolute deviation (MAD) for the sample data.

Calculating the MAD

Shown below is a procedure for calculating the mean absolute deviation on a TI-83 calculator. Follow this procedure using the sample data: 7, 3, 2, 5, 6, and 4.

1. First clear List 1 and enter the data into List 1.

2. Find the mean of the data in List 1 using 1-Var Stats from the STAT/CALC menu. The mean is $\bar{x}$.

3. To place the distance of each data value from the mean in List 2, first view the lists and then place the cursor on top of L_2.

4. Because the mean is 4.5, press MATH ▶ ENTER 2nd 1 − 4.5) ENTER. The command abs(L_1 − 4.5) removes any negative signs from the differences before they are stored in L_2; "abs" stands for absolute value.

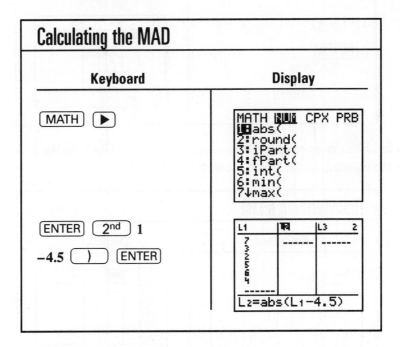

5. Use 1-Var Stats to get the average of L_2. This average is the mean absolute deviation (MAD) for the sample data.

Use with page 66.

Transforming Lists

Before starting Activity 2, clear Lists 1 and 2. Here is another method to clear lists. Use the arrow keys to highlight the L_1 column heading, then press [CLEAR] [ENTER]. You can use the same method to clear L_2 by highlighting L_2 instead of L_1.

Another Method to Clear Lists	
Keyboard	**Display**
[▲]	L1 | L2 | L3 7 | 2.5 3 | 1.5 2 | 2.5 5 | .5 6 | 1.5 4 | .5 ------ | ------ $L_1=\{7,3,2,5,6,4\}$
[CLEAR] [ENTER]	L1 | L2 | L3 ▬▬▬ | 2.5 | 1.5 | 2.5 | .5 | 1.5 | .5 ------ $L_1(1)=$

To *transform* the data in List L_1 and then store the new data in List L_2, highlight the L_2 column heading and complete the equation in the lower left with $L_2 = L_1 + 2$.

Transforming a List	
Keyboard	**Display**
[2nd] 1 + 2	L1 | L2 | L3 24.1 | ------ | ------ 26.5 19.9 20.7 22.4 21.3 24.8 $L_2=L_1+2$
[ENTER]	L1 | L2 | L3 24.1 | 26.1 | ------ 26.5 | 28.5 19.9 | 21.9 20.7 | 22.7 22.4 | 24.4 21.3 | 23.3 24.8 | 26.8 $L_2(1)=26.1$

MASTER 34

Transforming Lists

Before starting Activity 2, clear Lists 1 and 2. Here is another method to clear lists. Use the arrow keys to highlight the L_1 column heading, then press $\boxed{\text{CLEAR}}$ $\boxed{\text{ENTER}}$. You can use the same method to clear L_2 by highlighting L_2 instead of L_1.

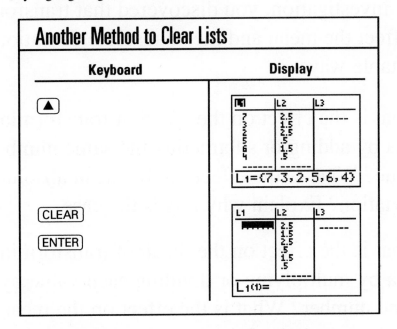

To *transform* the data in List L_1 and then store the new data in List L_2, highlight the L_2 column heading and complete the equation in the lower left with $L_2 = L_1 + 2$.

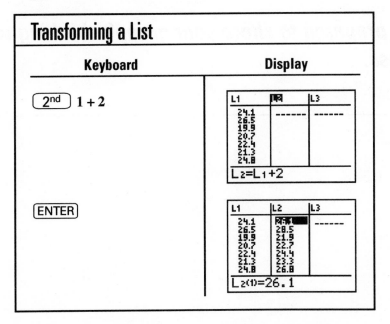

Use with page 66.

Checkpoint

In this investigation, you discovered that transformations of data affect the mean and mean absolute deviation in predictable ways.

a What is the effect on the mean of transforming a set of data by adding or subtracting the same number to each value? What is the effect on the mean absolute deviation? Explain why this is the case.

b What is the effect on the mean of transforming a set of data by multiplying or dividing each value by the same number? What is the effect on the mean absolute deviation?

Be prepared to share your group's thinking with the class.

Think About This Situation

Suppose you are interested primarily in interior space and cargo space for the cars in the $20,000–$25,000 range tested by the AAA. Examine the ratings (on page 74) of the tested cars on these two characteristics.

a According to the ratings, do the cars with the best interior space also have the best cargo space?

b Do the cars with the worst interior space also have the worst cargo space?

c In general, does it look like cars with better interior space have better cargo space and cars with poorer interior space have poorer cargo space?

d Does there have to be a compromise between interior space and cargo space?

Displaying a Scatterplot

To produce the scatterplot for Activity 3, first clear the data in lists L_1 and L_2. Enter the ratings for the Concorde in L_1 and those for the Intrepid in L_2. Set the viewing window as shown below.

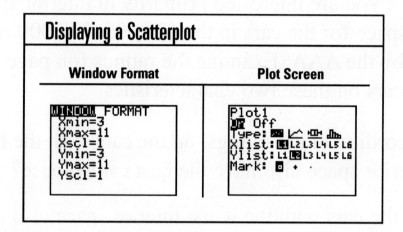

Displaying a Scatterplot

Window Format

```
WINDOW FORMAT
 Xmin=3
 Xmax=11
 Xscl=1
 Ymin=3
 Ymax=11
 Yscl=1
```

Plot Screen

```
Plot1
On Off
Type: ▦ ⌐ ◫ ⊞
Xlist: L1 L2 L3 L4 L5 L6
Ylist: L1 L2 L3 L4 L5 L6
Mark: □ + ·
```

Next, access the STAT PLOT menu and select Plot 1. Set the PLOT SCREEN as shown above. Note carefully how the Xlist and Ylist are specified.

Press [GRAPH] and the scatterplot of the ratings for the Concorde and Intrepid should appear in the viewing screen.

**MASTER
38**

Displaying a Scatterplot

To produce the scatterplot for Activity 3, first clear the data in lists L_1 and L_2. Enter the ratings for the Concorde in L_1 and those for the Intrepid in L_2. Set the viewing window as shown below.

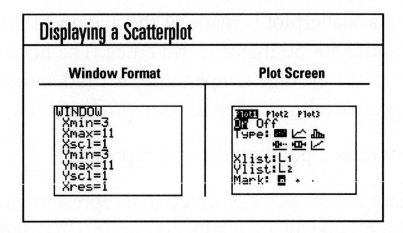

Displaying a Scatterplot

Window Format	Plot Screen
WINDOW Xmin=3 Xmax=11 Xscl=1 Ymin=3 Ymax=11 Yscl=1 Xres=1	Plot1 Plot2 Plot3 On Off Type: Xlist:L₁ Ylist:L₂ Mark: ■ + ·

Next, access the STAT PLOT menu and select Plot 1. Set the PLOT SCREEN as shown above. Note carefully how the Xlist and Ylist are specified.

Press $\boxed{\text{GRAPH}}$ and the scatterplot of the ratings for the Concorde and Intrepid should appear in the viewing screen.

Checkpoint

Suppose a scatterplot is made of the average 1990 and 2000 temperatures for 50 major world cities. The horizontal axis represents the average temperature in 1990 and the vertical axis represents the average temperature in 2000.

a What does a point on the plot represent?

b Where are the points located that represent cities that had the same average temperature in 1990 and 2000?

c How could you use the line $y = x$ to determine if temperatures generally increased from 1990 to 2000?

d Is it always helpful to draw in the line $y = x$ on a scatterplot? Why or why not?

Be prepared to share your group's responses with the whole class.

Displaying a Plot over Time

To produce a plot over time, proceed just as you did in producing a scatterplot, but select the **line plot** as the desired graph. In the particular case of Activity 4, first clear the data from lists L_1 and L_2. Enter the years *in order* in L_1 and the corresponding average repair ratings for the Mustang in L_2. Press $\boxed{\text{WINDOW}}$ and select appropriate minimum and maximum values for the axes. Use Xscl = 1 and Yscl = 0.25. Use the STAT PLOT menu to turn off all plots with the exception of Plot 1. For Plot 1, use the down arrow key to select Type, and use the right arrow key and $\boxed{\text{ENTER}}$ key to choose the second plot. Use the arrow and $\boxed{\text{ENTER}}$ keys to be sure that Xlist is L_1 and Ylist is L_2. Press $\boxed{\text{GRAPH}}$ and a time plot of the repair ratings of the Mustang should appear.

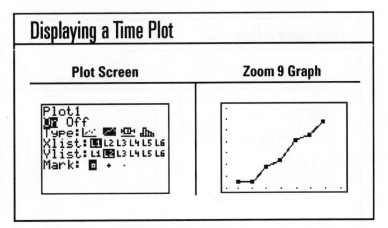

The Intrepid data include one more data point than the Mustang data. In order to compare the average repair ratings of the Mustang and Intrepid, the Intrepid data from 1993 should not be included. Enter the repair ratings for the Intrepid for 1994–2000 from the table on page 81 in list L_3. Turn Plot 2 on and then select the line plot. Select Xlist to be L_1 and Ylist to be L_3. Choose the + mark for the data points for the Intrepid. Set an appropriate viewing window. Press $\boxed{\text{GRAPH}}$, and you should see time plots for both of the ratings on the screen. If necessary, use ZoomStat ($\boxed{\text{ZOOM}}$ 9) to adjust the display.

Displaying a Plot over Time

To produce a plot over time, proceed just as you did in producing a scatterplot, but select the **line plot** as the desired graph. In the particular case of Activity 4, first clear the data from lists L_1 and L_2. Enter the years *in order* in L_1 and the corresponding average repair ratings for the Mustang in L_2. Press WINDOW and select appropriate minimum and maximum values for the axes. Use Xscl = 1 and Yscl = 0.25. Use the STAT PLOT menu to turn off all plots with the exception of Plot 1. For Plot 1, use the down arrow key to select Type, and use the right arrow key and ENTER key to choose the second plot. Use the arrow and ENTER keys to be sure that Xlist is L_1 and Ylist is L_2. Press GRAPH and a time plot of the repair ratings of the Mustang should appear.

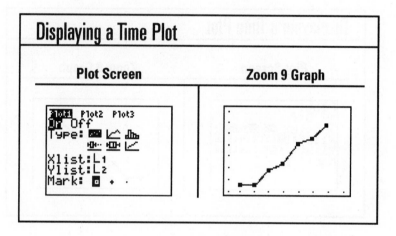

The Intrepid data include one more data point than the Mustang data. In order to compare the average repair ratings of the Mustang and Intrepid, the Intrepid data from 1993 should not be included. Enter the repair ratings for the Intrepid for 1994–2000 from the table on page 81 in list L_3. Turn Plot 2 on and then select the line plot. Select Xlist to be L_1 and Ylist to be L_3. Choose the + mark for the data points for the Intrepid. Set an appropriate viewing window. Press GRAPH, and you should see time plots for both of the ratings on the screen. If necessary, use ZoomStat (ZOOM 9) to adjust the display.

Use with page 82.

Checkpoint

In this investigation, you explored how to interpret and make a plot over time.

a Describe a plot over time.

b What information can you learn from a plot over time?

c How can you use a plot over time to find the time period when the least change occurs? The most?

d How can the scale on the axes affect your interpretation of a plot over time?

Be prepared to share your group's thinking on the interpretation of plots over time.

Climate of World Cities

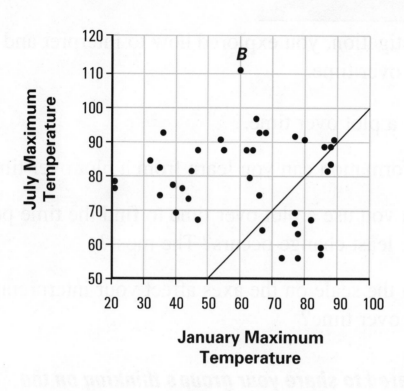

January Maximum Temperature

(y-axis) July Maximum Temperature

**MASTER
44**

Climate of World Cities

City	Ave. January Temperature (in °F)		Ave. July Temperature (in °F)	
	Maximum	**Minimum**	**Maximum**	**Minimum**
Accra, Ghana	87	73	81	73
Amsterdam, Netherlands	40	34	69	59
Athens, Greece	54	42	90	72
Auckland, New Zealand	73	60	56	46
Baghdad, Iraq	60	39	110	76
Bangkok, Thailand	89	67	90	76
Beirut, Lebanon	62	51	87	73
Berlin, Germany	35	26	74	55
Bogota, Columbia	67	48	64	50
Bombay, India	88	62	88	75
Budapest, Hungary	35	26	82	61
Buenos Aires, Argentina	85	63	57	42
Cairo, Egypt	65	47	96	70
Calcutta, India	80	55	90	79
Cape Town, South Africa	78	60	63	45
Casablanca, Morocco	63	45	79	65
Dublin, Ireland	47	35	67	51
Geneva, Switzerland	39	29	77	58
Hanoi, Vietnam	68	58	92	79
Hong Kong	64	56	87	78
Istanbul, Turkey	45	36	81	65
Jerusalem, Israel	55	41	87	63
Kabul, Afghanistan	36	18	92	61
Karachi, Pakistan	77	55	91	81
Lagos, Nigeria	88	74	83	74
Lima, Peru	82	66	67	57
London, UK	44	35	73	55
Madrid, Spain	47	33	87	62
Manila, Philippines	86	69	88	75
Melbourne, Australia	78	57	56	42
Mexico City, Mexico	66	42	74	54
Montreal, Canada	21	6	78	61
Moscow, Russia	21	9	76	55
Nairobi, Kenya	77	54	69	51
Osaka, Japan	47	32	87	73
Paris, France	42	32	76	55
Santiago, Chile	85	53	59	37
Sao Paulo, Brazil	77	63	66	53
Seoul, South Korea	32	15	84	70
Taipei, Taiwan	66	53	92	76

Source: *The New York Times 2001 Almanac.* New York, NY: The New York Times Company, 2000.

Use with page 91.

Checkpoint

Patterns in data can be seen in graphical displays of the distribution and can be summarized using measures of center and variability.

a Describe the kinds of information you can get by examining

- a stem-and-leaf plot;
- a number line plot or histogram;
- a box plot;
- a scatterplot;
- a plot over time.

b Describe the kinds of situations for which each plot is most useful.

c How do you decide which measure of center to use to provide a summary of a distribution? How do you decide on which measure of variability to report?

d Which measures of center and of variability are readily found from the graphical displays you studied?

Be prepared to share your group's descriptions and thinking with the entire class.

Think About This Situation

Suppose the Five Star Amusement Park intends to set up a bungee jump.

a How could they design the bungee jump so that people of different weights could all have safe but exciting jumps?

b What patterns would you expect in a table or graph showing the expected stretch of a 50-foot bungee cord with different weights?

Jumper Weight (in pounds)	Cord Stretch (in feet)
50	?
100	
150	
200	
250	

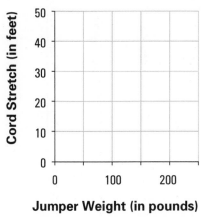

c How could they find the price to charge for each jump so the park could maximize profit?

d What other safety and business problems would Five Star have to consider to set up and operate the new bungee attraction safely and profitably?

Modeling a Bungee Apparatus

Weight	Amount of Stretch

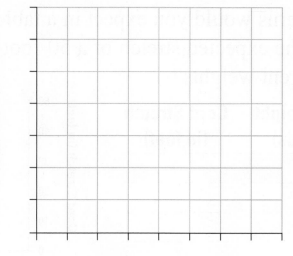

Stretch of Model Cord

Weight of Model Jumper

Checkpoint

Data from experiments often suggest possible relationships between variables.

a What are the important variables in the design of a bungee apparatus?

b When change in one variable is related to change in another variable, the pattern of that relation can be described in *words*, with a *table* of sample data, or with a *graph* of sample data. What are the advantages and disadvantages of describing patterns of change in related variables by each of these methods?

Be prepared to share your group's thinking with the whole class.

Think About This Situation

The population of our world changes rapidly—in 15 years it is expected to grow by over one billion people.

a What are some of the major factors that might influence population change in a country?

b Why would it be important to know year-to-year population changes, and how you could estimate those changes without a full census survey?

Checkpoint

In population studies of Brazil and the United States, you made estimates for several years, based on growth trends from the past.

a What calculations are needed to estimate population growth from one year to the next in the two different countries?

b Using the word *NOW* to stand for the population of the United States in any year, write an expression that shows how to calculate the population in the *NEXT* year.

Be prepared to compare your expression relating **NOW** *and* **NEXT** *with those of other groups.*

Checkpoint

In this study of whale populations, you again made estimates for several years, based on growth trends from the past.

a What calculations must you do to estimate the change in number of whales from one year to the next?

b Explain how to use your technology's "last answer" function to calculate the total population in the next year.

c Explain how your calculator or computer software can be used to predict the total population many years ahead.

Be prepared to share your procedures with the entire class.

Time Worked (in hours)	0	1	2	3	4	5	10	15
Money Earned (in dollars)	0	5.25	10.50	15.75	21.00	26.25	52.50	78.75

Think About This Situation

The table shows money earned for a sample of hours worked. But the payroll computer for a company with many workers will have to be able to calculate pay for any number of hours.

a In this case, pay increases by $5.25 from one hour to the next. Using the words *NOW* and *NEXT*, how could you write that rule with an equation that begins
$NEXT =$ _____ ?

b Using the letters H (for number of hours worked) and E (for number of dollars earned), how could you write a rule that gives earnings for *any* number of hours worked with an equation that begins $E =$ _____ ?

c How could you calculate the money earned for any number of hours worked, such as 23 or 42, and for fractions of hours, such as 8.25 hours or 12.5 hours?

d Why might rules like those called for in Parts a or b be more useful than tables or graphs of the (*time worked*, *pay earned*) data?

Number of Payments	Unpaid Balance (in dollars)
0	_____
1	_____
2	_____
3	_____
4	_____
5	_____
6	_____
7	_____
8	_____
9	_____
10	_____

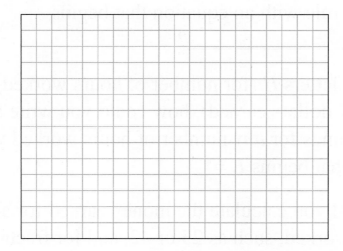

Palace Theater Income Data

Number of Tickets Sold	Income (in dollars)
0	
50	
100	
150	
200	
250	
300	

Palace Theater Profit Data

Number of Tickets Sold	Profit (in dollars)
0	
50	
100	
150	
200	
250	
300	

Tickets and Income

Regular Tickets	Discount Tickets	Income (in dollars)
100	100	
200	100	
100	200	
150	250	
250	150	

Tickets and Profit

Regular Tickets	Discount Tickets	Profit (in dollars)
100	100	
200	100	
100	200	
150	250	
250	150	

Checkpoint

The earnings, installment buying, and Palace Theater situations all involved variables that changed in relation to each other.

a Describe the variables involved and the patterns of change in each case.

b Explain how the patterns are similar and how they are different.

c How are the graphs similar and how are they different?

d Write at least two rules that you determined in this investigation. What is the relationship between patterns and rules?

Be prepared to share your group's descriptions and observations with the class.

Creating Graphs with TablePlot

TablePlot software for your calculator links the making of tables and graphs to a function rule. The basic steps in using this software are summarized below.

Using TBLPLOT

Enter Rule	Setup Table	Select Table or Graph

```
Y₁="2.50X-450




REMEMBER: START
WITH A QUOTATION
MARK (ALPHA +)
```

```
TABLE VALUES
1:Y₁ IS ON
2:Y₂ IS OFF
3:TblMin=0
4:ΔTbl=20
5:TblMaX=200
[6]RETURN
```

```
DISPLAY MENU
1:VIEW TABLE
2:VIEW GRAPH
3:EDIT VALUES
4:EDIT RULES
5:MAIN MENU
```

Creating Graphs with TablePlot

TablePlot software for your calculator links the making of tables and graphs to a function rule. The basic steps in using this software are summarized below.

Using TBLPLOT

Enter Rule	Setup Table	Select Table or Graph
Y₁= 2.50X−450	TABLE VALUES 1:Y₁ IS ON 2:Y₂ IS OFF 3:TblStart=0 4:ΔTbl=20 5:TblEnd=200 [6]RETURN	DISPLAY MENU 1:VIEW TABLE 2:VIEW GRAPH 3:EDIT VALUES 4:EDIT RULES 5:MAIN MENU

Checkpoint

Suppose a cross-country bus travels at an average speed of 50 miles per hour.

ⓐ Describe two ways to use a calculator or computer to produce a table of values showing how far that bus travels as a function of time during the trip. What are the advantages or disadvantages of each method?

ⓑ Describe two ways to use a calculator or computer to graph the relation between time and distance. What are the advantages or disadvantages of each method?

ⓒ Write and answer three different questions that can be answered using the table or the graph.

Be prepared to share your questions and methods with the class.

Think About This Situation

Suppose you threw a ball straight up into the air at a velocity of 25 meters per second. (Major league pitches travel approximately 95 miles per hour, which is about 42.5 meters per second.)

a About how high do you think the ball would go before it starts falling back to the ground?

b About how many seconds do you think it would take before the ball hits the ground?

c Which of the following graphs do you think best matches the pattern of (*time*, *height*) data describing the ball's flight? Explain your choice.

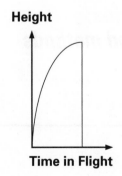

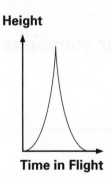

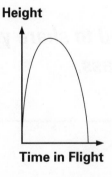

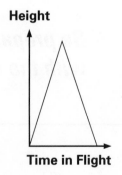

Checkpoint

As you worked on questions about the baseball's flight, how did you use your calculator or computer to find:

a the maximum height and the time it took the ball to reach that height?

b the time the ball returned to the ground and the speed it was traveling when it hit?

Be prepared to share your group's methods with the whole class.

MASTER
61a

Experiment 1

a. $y = 2x - 4$

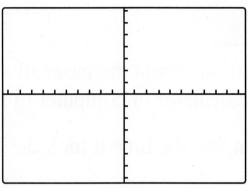

Window _____

x	*y*
___	___
___	___
___	___
___	___
___	___
___	___
___	___

b. $y = 2x + 4$

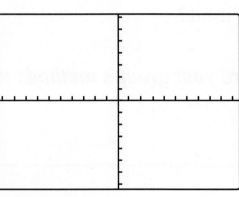

Window _____

x	*y*
___	___
___	___
___	___
___	___
___	___
___	___
___	___
___	___
___	___

c. $y = 0.5x + 2$

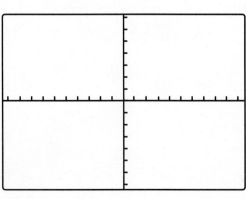

Window _____

x	*y*
___	___
___	___
___	___
___	___
___	___
___	___
___	___

MASTER 61b

Experiment 1 *(continued)*

d. $y = -0.5x + 2$

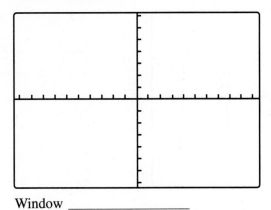

Window _____

x	y

e. $y = 10 - 1.5x$

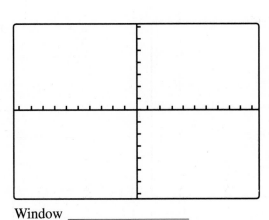

Window _____

x	y

f. $y = x^2 - 4$

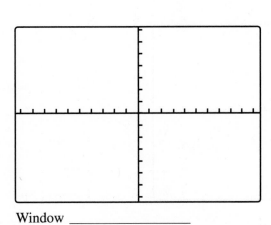

Window _____

x	y

MASTER
62a

Experiment 2

a. $y = x^2$

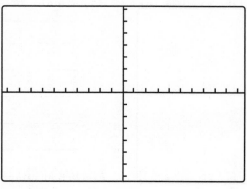

Window _____

x	y

b. $y = x^2 - 3$

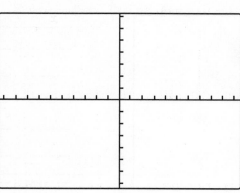

Window _____

x	y

c. $y = -x^2$

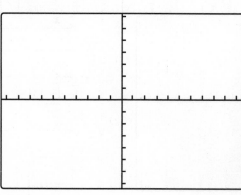

Window _____

x	y

Experiment 2 *(continued)*

d. $y = -x^2 + 5$

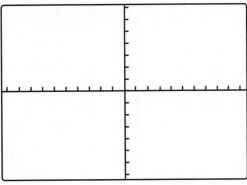

Window _____

x	y

e. $y = (x + 3)^2$

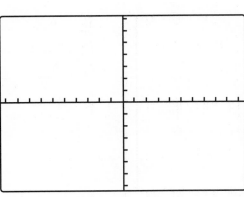

Window _____

x	y

f. $y = \frac{2}{x}$

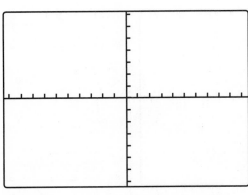

Window _____

x	y

Use with page 145.

Experiment 3

a. $y = \frac{1}{x}$

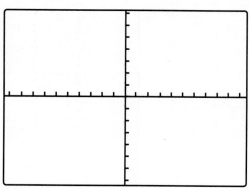

Window _____

x	y

b. $y = \frac{3}{x}$

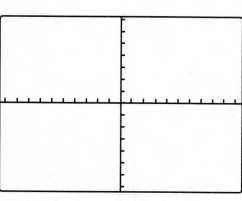

Window _____

x	y

c. $y = \frac{5}{x}$

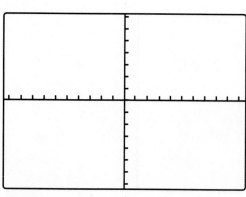

Window _____

x	y

Experiment 3 *(continued)*

d. $y = \dfrac{-5}{x}$

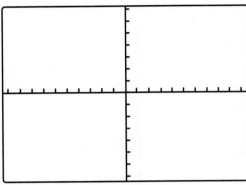

Window _____

x	y

e. $y = \dfrac{5}{x + 1}$

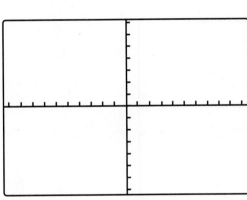

Window _____

x	y

f. $y = \dfrac{x}{3}$

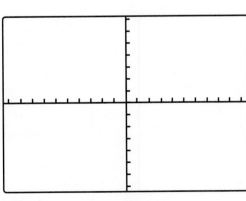

Window _____

x	y

MASTER
64a

Experiment 4

a. $y = 2^x$

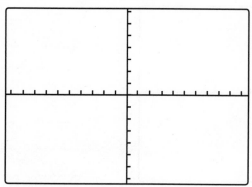

Window _____

x	y

b. $y = (1.5)^x$

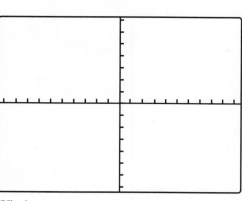

Window _____

x	y

c. $y = 3^x$

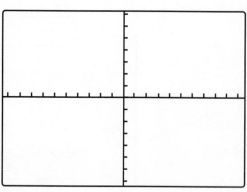

Window _____

x	y

Experiment 4 *(continued)*

d. $y = x^3$

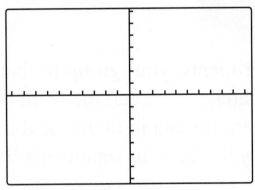

Window _____

x	y

e. $y = (0.5)^x$

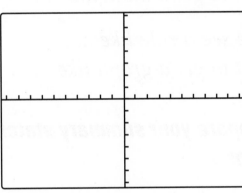

Window _____

x	y

f. $y = x^{0.5}$

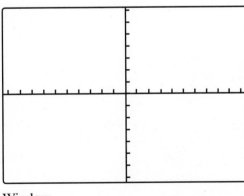

Window _____

x	y

Use with page 146.

Checkpoint

As a result of the experiments, your group probably has some hunches about matches between the form of a symbolic rule, the pattern of data in tables, and the shape of graphs. Summarize your ideas in statements like this:

If we see a rule like ... ,
we expect to get a table like ... .

If we see a rule like ... ,
we expect to get a graph like ... .

Be prepared to compare your summary statements with those of other groups.

Checkpoint

When two variables change in relation to each other, the pattern of change often fits one of several common forms.

a Make sketches of at least five different graphs showing different patterns relating change in two variables.

b For each graph, write a brief explanation of the pattern of change shown in the graph and describe a real-life situation that fits the pattern.

Be prepared to share your sketches and descriptions with the whole class.

Flag and Shadow Display

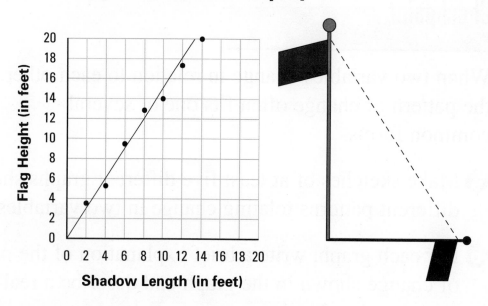

Think About This Situation

As in many experiments, the shadow data do not fall exactly on a line. No simple equation will relate all of the (*shadow length*, *flag height*) data pairs.

a How would you decide where to draw a line fitting the pattern in a plot like the one above?

b What predictions could you make from the given linear model?

c What kinds of equations do you expect for linear graphs?

Checkpoint

The relationship between projector distance and enlargement factor can be represented by a linear model, which can then be used to make predictions.

a Suppose you were to draw one line segment on an overhead transparency. The relation between the length of the screen image of that segment and the distance the projector lens is from the screen can be represented by a data table, a graph model, or an equation. Which representation do you think is easiest to use and most accurate for making predictions? Give reasons for your choice.

b What factors could cause inaccurate predictions from a linear model of (*projector distance*, *enlargement factor*) data?

Be prepared to share your group's responses with the entire class.

Television Ratings Display

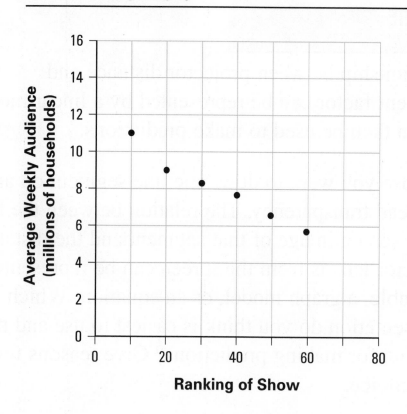

TV Ratings

Rank	Show	Audience Size
1	ER, NBC	17.5
2	Survivor II, CBS	16.6
3	CSI: Crime Scene Investigation, CBS	14.4
4	Who Wants to Be a Millionaire-Sunday, ABC	12.0
5	The West Wing, NBC	11.9
6	Who Wants to Be a Millionaire-Tuesday, ABC	11.7
7	Everybody Loves Raymond, CBS	11.4
8	Law and Order, NBC	11.3
9	The Practice, ABC	11.2
10	Friends, NBC	10.9
11	Will & Grace, NBC	10.5
12	Becker, CBS	10.2
	Just Shoot Me, NBC	10.2
14	Who Wants to Be a Millionaire-Thursday, ABC	9.9
15	Law and Order: Special Victim's Unit, NBC	9.7
16	NYPD Blue, ABC	9.6
17	Who Wants to Be a Millionaire-Friday, ABC	9.5
18	Judging Amy, CBS	9.4
	Weakest Link, NBC	9.4
20	60 Minutes, CBS	9.1
21	CSI: Crime Scene Investigation-Friday, CBS	8.9
	Dharma & Greg, ABC	8.9
	The District, CBS	8.9
24	20/20 Friday, ABC	8.8
	JAG, CBS	8.8
	Third Watch, NBC	8.8
	Touched By an Angel, CBS	8.8
28	CBS Sunday Movie: On Golden Pond, CBS	8.7
29	NBC Sunday Night Movie: U.S. Marshals, NBC	8.6
30	Simpsons, Fox	8.4

Rank	Show	Audience Size
31	48 Hours-Monday, CBS	8.3
	60 Minutes II, CBS	8.3
33	Providence, NBC	8.2
34	Malcolm in the Middle, Fox	8.1
35	Ally McBeal, Fox	8.0
36	My Wife & Kids-8:30pm, ABC	7.9
	The Weber Show, NBC	7.9
38	What About Joan, ABC	7.8
39	Frasier, NBC	7.7
40	Dateline NBC-Monday, NBC	7.6
41	The X-Files, Fox	7.4
42	Diagnosis Murder, CBS	7.2
	My Wife & Kids-8:00pm, ABC	7.2
44	Boston Public, Fox	7.1
45	Dateline NBC-Friday, NBC	7.0
	Walker, Texas Ranger, CBS	7.0
47	Dateline NBC-Tuesday, NBC	6.9
48	48 Hours, CBS	6.8
49	Boot Camp, Fox	6.7
	The Drew Carey Show, ABC	6.7
	King of Queens, CBS	6.7
52	Nash Bridges, CBS	6.5
	Yes, Dear, CBS	6.5
54	Once and Again, ABC	6.4
55	Primetime Thursday, ABC	6.2
56	Simpsons Special, Fox	6.1
57	Dark Angel, Fox	6.0
58	Wonderful World of Disney: Tarzan, ABC	5.9
59	Ed, NBC	5.8
	That '70s Show, Fox	5.8
	Three Sisters, NBC	5.8
	Walker, Texas Ranger-8:00pm, CBS	5.8
63	Spin City, ABC	5.7
64	America's Most Wanted: America Fights Back, Fox	5.5
	Titus, Fox	5.5

TV Ratings (*continued*)

Rank	Show	Audience Size
66	That '70s Show 2, Fox	5.2
67	ABC Saturday Night Movie: Meet Joe Black, ABC	5.1
	Vanished: Shooting Star, ABC	5.1
69	CBS Wednesday Movie: Contact, CBS	5.0
	Cops 2: Seattle/Tacoma, Fox	5.0
	Grounded For Life, Fox	5.0
	Simpsons-Sunday, Fox	5.0
73	In Style: Celebrity Moms, NBC	4.9
74	NBC Saturday Night Movie: Goldeneye, NBC	4.6
75	ABC Monday Night Movie: Kiss My Act, ABC	4.4
	World's Worst Drivers: Caught 3, Fox	4.4
77	7th Heaven, WB	4.3
	Surviving Moment Impact 4, Fox	4.3
	Whose Line is it Anyway?- 8:30pm, ABC	4.3
80	Cops: Arizona, Fox	4.2
	Police Videos, Fox	4.2
82	World Wrestling Federation Smackdown!, UPN	3.7
83	Whose Line is it Anyway?- Friday 8:00pm, ABC	3.6
	Whose Line is it Anyway?- Friday 8:30pm, ABC	3.6
85	Whose Line is it Anyway?, ABC	3.3
86	Dawson's Creek-WB, WB	3.1
87	Buffy, the Vampire Slayer, WB	3.0
	Star Trek: Voyager, UPN	3.0
89	Angel, WB	2.8
90	Roswell, WB	2.6
91	Charmed, WB	2.5
	Gilmore Girls, WB	2.5
	Lone Gunmen, Fox	2.5
	UPN's Movie Friday: The Fifth Element, UPN	2.5
95	Felicity-WB, WB	2.4
96	The Parkers, UPN	2.2

Rank	Show	Audience Size
97	Hughleys, The, UPN	2.1
	Moesha, UPN	2.1
99	Girlfriends, UPN	2.0
100	Nikki, WB	1.8
	Special Unit 2, UPN	1.8
102	Chains of Love, UPN	1.7
	For Your Love, WB	1.7
	The Steve Harvey Show, WB	1.7
105	Oblongs, WB	1.6
	Sabrina, the Teenage Witch- 8:00pm, WB	1.6
107	Sabrina, the Teenage Witch- 8:30pm, WB	1.4
108	Diagnosis Murder-Thursday, PAX	1.3
	Diagnosis Murder-Tuesday, PAX	1.3
	Diagnosis Murder-Wednesday, PAX	1.3
	Doc, PAX	1.3
	Doc Enc, PAX	1.3
	Touched By an Angel- Wednesday, PAX	1.3
114	Popular, WB	1.2
115	Joseph of Nazareth: Joseph Of Nazareth, PAX	1.1
	The PJs, WB	1.1
117	All Souls, UPN	1.0
	Candid Camera-7:30pm, PAX	1.0
	Diagnosis Murder Sp 4/27, PAX	1.0
	Popstars, WB	1.0
121	Miracle Pets, PAX	0.9
	Nothing Lasts Forever Part 2, PAX	0.9
123	Mysterious Ways, PAX	0.8
124	Candid Camera-7:00pm, PAX	0.7
	Candid Camera-Saturday, PAX	0.7
	It's a Miracle, PAX	0.7
127	Encounters With the Unexplained, PAX	0.6
	Miracle Pets Encore, PAX	0.6
	Touched By an Angel- Saturday, PAX	0.6
	Twice in a Lifetime, PAX	0.6
131	Mysterious Ways Encore, PAX	0.5

Checkpoint

In Investigations 1 and 2 of this lesson, you used tables and graphs of sample (x, y) data pairs to find a line that would fit all data in a collection reasonably well.

a How do you use a modeling line to estimate y values related to any of the chosen x values?

b How do you use a modeling line to estimate the x values that will predict any chosen y value?

Be prepared to share your group's procedures with the whole class.

**MASTER
72**

Activity Master

Tuition Costs

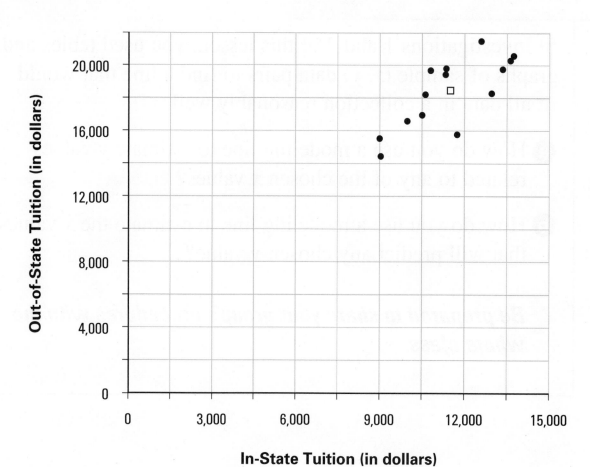

**MASTER
73**

Mean Absolute Error

Predicting from $y = x + 1$

x	Actual y	Predicted from $y = x + 1$	Error Actual – Predicted	Absolute Error
0	2	1	1	1
1	2	2	0	0
2	3			
3	5			
4	5			
5	6			
7	7			
7	8			
8	9			
9	9	10	– 1	1

Mean absolute error = _____

Predicting from $y = 0.7x + 2.38$

x	Actual y	Predicted from $y = 0.7x + 2.38$	Error Actual – Predicted	Absolute Error
0	2	2.38	– 0.38	0.38
1	2	3.08	– 1.08	1.08
2	3			
3	5			
4	5			
5	6			
7	7			
7	8			
8	9			
9	9			

Mean absolute error = _____

Use with page 168.

Checkpoint

In this investigation, you considered the problem of choosing the best linear models for given data patterns.

a What strategies seem sensible in finding a good linear model?

b If two different linear models are proposed, how could you compare them to see which is the better fit to the data pattern?

Be prepared to share your strategies and reasoning with the class.

High Temperature vs. Boogie Boards

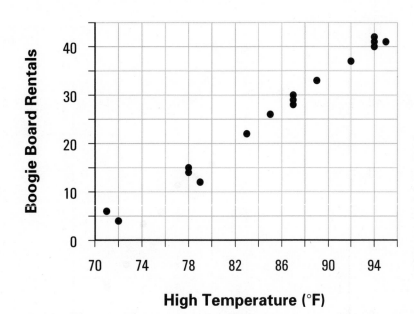

Helicopter Market Survey

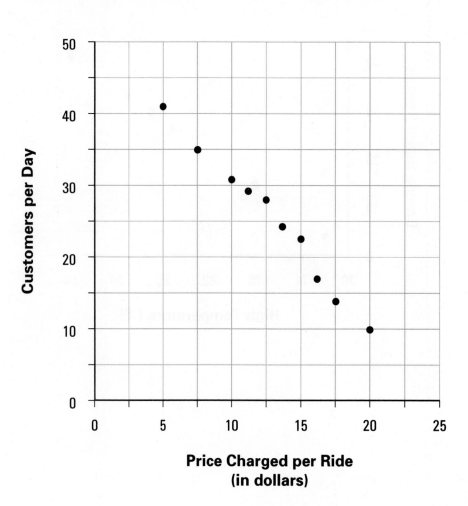

Rubber Band Bungee Display

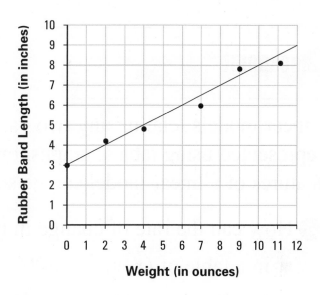

Think About This Situation

The graph shows the overall pattern relating *weight* and rubber band *length*.

a Based on the linear model (not the data points themselves), what pattern would you expect in a table of (*weight*, *length*) data pairs for weights that range from 0 to 10 ounces?

b How long is this rubber band with no weight attached, and how is that fact shown on the graph?

c How much does the rubber band stretch for each ounce of weight added, and how is that shown on the graph?

Use with page 181.

Checkpoint

Linear models relating any two variables x and y can be represented using tables, graphs, or equations. Important features of a linear model can be seen in each representation.

a How can the rate of change in two variables be seen:

- in a table of (x, y) values?

- in a linear graph?

- in an equation relating *NOW* and *NEXT* for the model?

- in an equation relating x and y?

b How can the *y*-intercept be seen:

- in a table of (x, y) values?

- in a linear graph?

- in an equation relating *NOW* and *NEXT* for the model?

- in an equation relating x and y?

Be prepared to share your group's descriptions with the whole class.

Finding a Linear Regression Line

To compute the slope and *y*-intercept of the LinReg model for data in your lists, press $\boxed{\text{STAT}}$, select CALC, and then choose option 9: LinReg ($a + bx$). Indicate the appropriate lists for the independent variable and the dependent variable. The key sequence is summarized as follows.

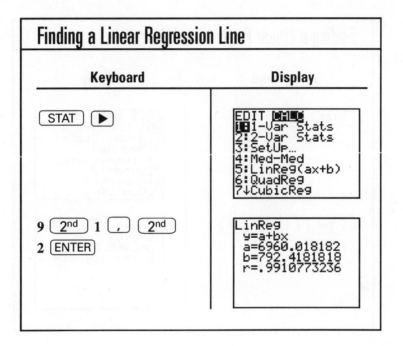

Note that the calculator uses b for the slope and a for the *y*-intercept for $y = a + bx$.

Finding a Linear Regression Line

To compute the slope and *y*-intercept of the LinReg model for data in your lists, press [STAT], select CALC, and then choose option 8: LinReg (*a* + *bx*). Indicate the appropriate lists for the independent variable and the dependent variable. The key sequence is summarized as follows.

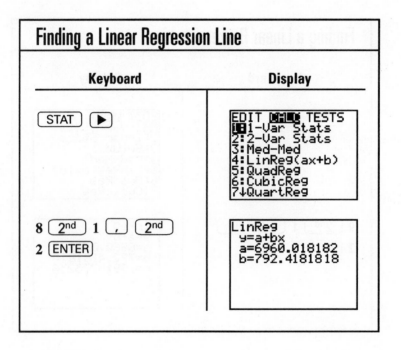

Note that the calculator uses *b* for the slope and *a* for the *y*-intercept for *y* = *a* + *bx*.

Checkpoint

There are several different methods of finding an equation for a linear model.

a To find an equation in the form $y = a + bx$, how can you use information about:

- slope and y-intercept of the graph of that model?

- rate of change and other values in a table of (x, y) data?

b How can you find the equation if slope and y-intercept are not given?

c In what cases does it make sense to use a graphing calculator or computer software to find the modeling line and equation? What steps are involved?

Be prepared to share descriptions of your methods with the entire class.

Checkpoint

How can the equation of a linear model be used to predict:

a the slope and location of its graph?

b the rate of change in a table of the equation's values?

Be prepared to share your group's thinking with the entire class.

Think About This Situation

The graph on page 211 shows trends in the numbers of male and female medical doctors in the United States between 1960 and 2000.

ⓐ How would you describe the trends shown in the data points and the linear models that have been drawn to match patterns in those points?

ⓑ Why do you suppose the percent of women doctors has been increasing over the past 40 years?

ⓒ Would you expect the trend in the graph to continue 10 or 20 years into the future? This means 10 or 20 years beyond 2000.

ⓓ How would you go about finding equations for linear models of the data trends?

ⓔ If you were asked to make a report on future prospects for numbers of male and female doctors, what kinds of questions could you answer using the linear models?

Checkpoint

Many important questions about linear models require solution of linear equations or inequalities, such as $50 = 23 + 5.2X$ or $45 - 3.5X < 25$.

a What does it mean to solve an equation or inequality?

b How do you check a solution?

c How could you use tables and graphs of linear models to solve the following equation and inequality:

- $50 = 23 + 5.2X$?
- $45 - 3.5X < 25$?

Be prepared to share your ideas with the class.

Checkpoint

It is often relatively easy to solve problems involving linear equations without the use of tables or graphs.

ⓐ Suppose you are going to tell someone how to solve an equation like $43 = 7 - 4x$ without use of a table or graph. What steps would you recommend? Why?

ⓑ When would you recommend solving an equation like the ones you've seen so far without a table or graph? When would you advise use of the calculator methods?

Be prepared to explain and defend your procedures.

Checkpoint

In solving a system of linear equations like $y = 5x + 8$ and $y = -3x + 14$, be able to answer the following questions:

a What is the objective?

b How could the solution be found on a graph of the two equations?

c How could the solution be found in a table of (x, y) values for both equations?

d How could the solution be found using reasoning with the symbolic forms themselves?

e What patterns in the tables, graphs, and equations of a system will indicate that there is no pair of values for x and y that satisfy both equations?

Be prepared to explain your solution methods and reasoning.

Checkpoint

In many situations, two people can suggest rules for linear models that are equivalent, but look quite different. For example, these two symbolic expressions for linear models are equivalent:

$$y = 15x - (12 + 7x) \text{ and } y = 8x - 12$$

a How could you test the equivalence using tables of (x, y) values?

b How could you test the equivalence using graphs of the relations?

c What reasoning with the symbolic forms alone would confirm the equivalence of the expressions?

Be prepared to explain your responses to the entire class.

Checkpoint

Linear patterns in data and linear relationships between quantities can be recognized in graphs, tables, and symbolic rules, or in conditions stated as applications or problems.

a Describe how you can tell whether a situation can be (or is) represented by a linear model by looking at:

- a scatterplot;
- a table of values;
- the form of the modeling equation;
- a description of the problem.

b Linear models often describe relationships between an input variable x and an output variable y.

- Write a general form for the rule of a linear model. What do the parts of the equation tell you about the relation being modeled?
- Explain how to find a value of y corresponding to a given value of x, using: **i.** a graph; **ii.** a table; **iii.** a symbolic rule.
- Explain how you can solve a linear equation using: **i.** a graph; **ii.** a table; **iii.** symbolic reasoning.
- Explain how you can solve a system of linear equations using: **i.** a graph; **ii.** a table; **iii.** symbolic reasoning.

Be prepared to share your descriptions and explanations with the whole class.

1. In the *Linear Models* unit you investigated bungee jumping and other situations involving springs and rubber bands. For example, the equation modeling one rubber band stretching experiment is $L = 2W + 6$, where L is length in inches for a weight W in ounces.

   a. Find the original length of rubber band.

   b. Find the length if the weight is 4.3 ounces.

   c. Find the weight if the length is 11.5 inches.

   d. What is the rate of change for this linear model? Explain what it means in terms of the weight of the springs and the stretch length of the rubber band.

Problems 2–4 could have arisen in other contexts.

2. Find the slope and y-intercept of:

   a. each line whose equation is given below.

      i. $y = 2.1 - 3.4x$

      ii. $2y = 5 + 6x$

   b. the line whose graph is shown at the right.

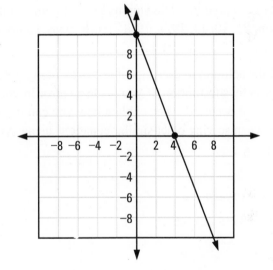

   c. the line whose table is shown at the right.

X	Y_1	
-5	-25	
-3	-17	
-1	-9	
1	-1	
3	7	
5	15	
7	23	
X= -5		

   d. the line given by $NEXT = NOW + 3.4$, starting at 2.

3. Find the equation of the line satisfying the given conditions.

   a. The slope is 4 and the line contains the point (3, 9).

   b. The line contains the points (1, 5) and (4, –3).

4. Rewrite each expression in an equivalent form.

   a. $8 - 2A + 3A - 16$

   b. $4.7x + 1 - 3x + 2$

   c. $4(y + 3)$

   d. $2(3x - 1)$

   e. $(2P - 5) - (3P + 7)$

5. McBride scored the following number of points in the first seven basketball games of the season: 21, 10, 14, 19, 8, 19, 12. How many points must she score in the eighth game to have a mean of 15 points per game?

6. Find the solution to each equation by reasoning with the symbolic form itself. Check your solution by substitution. If you made an error in your symbolic reasoning, determine where your error occurred. Then explain how you can minimize the chance of repeating the same error when solving other similar equations using symbolic reasoning.

   a. $24 = 6 + 2x$

   b. $63 = -2x - 11$

   c. $3(x + 12) = 9$

   d. $4P - (12 + 2P) = 6$

Suggested Solutions

1. a. The original length of the rubber band is 6 inches.

    b. If the weight is 4.3 ounces, then the length is 2(4.3) + 6 or 14.6 inches.

    c. If the length is 11.5 inches, then the weight is 2.75 ounces.

    d. It stretches 2 more inches for each additional ounce.

2. a. i. The slope is –3.4 and the y-intercept is 2.1.

      ii. The slope is 3 and the y-intercept is 2.5.

    b. The slope is –2.5 and the y-intercept is 10.

    c. The slope is 4 and the y-intercept is –5.

    d. The slope is 3.4 and the y-intercept is 2.

3. a. $y = 4x - 3$

    b. $y = -\frac{8}{3}x + \frac{23}{3}$

4. Responses may vary since students are asked for an equivalent form.

    a. $A - 8$

    b. $1.7x + 3$

    c. $4y + 12$

    d. $6x - 2$

    e. $-P - 12$

5. McBride must score 17 points in the eighth game.

6. a. $x = 9$

    b. $x = -37$

    c. $x = -9$

    d. $P = 9$

Think About This Situation

Suppose you have a job with a local school district for the summer. Your first assignment is to paint all the lockers in the high school.

a What are some tasks that would need to be completed before you could begin the actual painting?

b Would some tasks need to be completed before others? If so, in what order should the tasks be completed?

c Sketch a diagram of the arrangement of the lockers on one floor of your school.

d In what order would you paint the lockers? Do you think your plan involves the most efficient procedure? Why or why not?

Checkpoint

In this investigation, you saw how special diagrams consisting of points and connecting segments and arcs can be used to model situations in which an efficient route is to be found.

a What is the difference between a floor-plan map of a school showing the lockers to be painted and a mathematical model of the locker-painting problem?

b Refer back to Deonna's model. What do the points and the connecting segments and arcs represent in terms of the locker-painting problem?

c Can two diagrams that have different shapes and sizes represent the same problem situation? Explain.

d In Activity 2, you wrote a list of criteria for an optimal locker-painting plan. Restate those criteria in terms of tracing around a diagram that models the situation.

Be prepared to share your thinking with the entire class.

Making the Circuit

i.

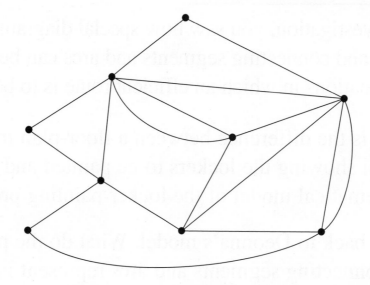

ii.

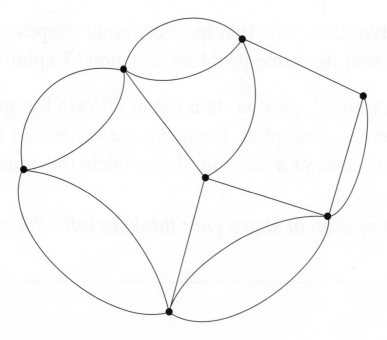

Making the Circuit

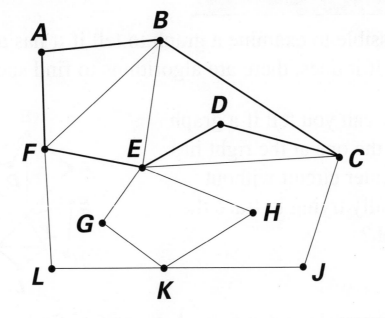

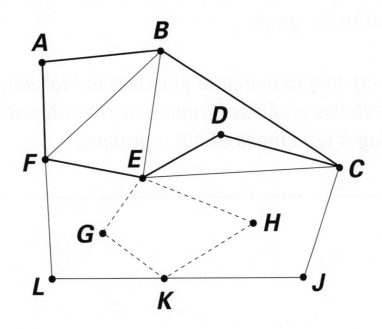

Checkpoint

It is possible to examine a graph to tell if it has an Euler circuit. If it does, there are algorithms to find such a circuit.

a How can you tell if a graph like the one at the right has an Euler circuit without actually trying to trace the graph?

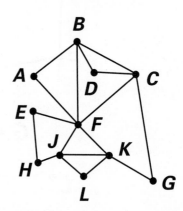

b Use your algorithm from Activity 6 to find an Euler circuit in the graph.

Be prepared to compare your method for determining if a graph has an Euler circuit and your algorithm for finding it with those of other groups.

**MASTER
95**

Metal Cut

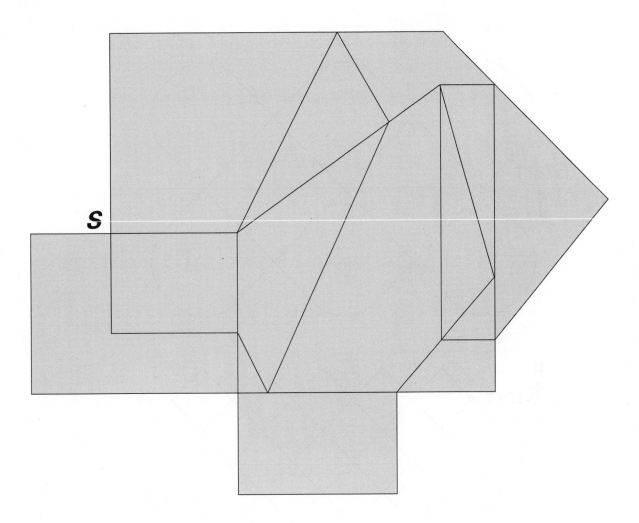

S

Tracing Figures from One Point to Another

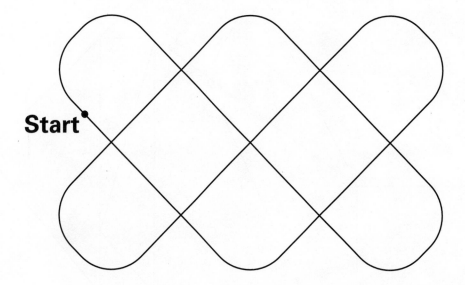

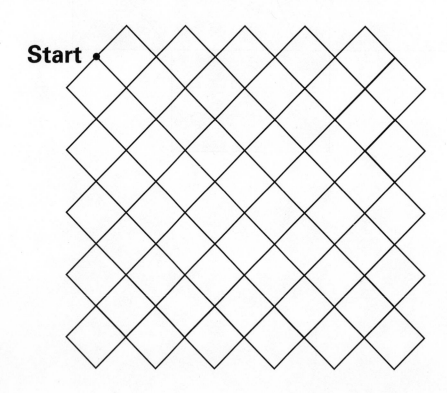

Tracing Figures from One Point to Another

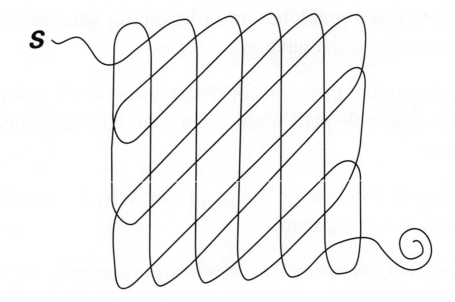

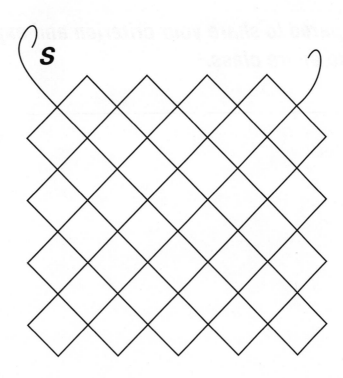

Checkpoint

You know that a graph has an Euler circuit whenever all vertices of the graph have even degree.

a Find a similar criterion for determining whether a graph *has* a traceable path when it does *not* have an Euler circuit.

b Test your criterion on the graphs in Activity 3 and on a graph that you create.

c Write an explanation for why your criterion is correct.

Be prepared to share your criterion and explanation with the entire class.

Checkpoint

A graph that does not have an Euler circuit can be Eulerized by adding appropriate edges.

a As a group, write an algorithm to Eulerize a graph.

b Test your algorithm by Eulerizing the graph shown here.

Be prepared to compare your algorithm with those of other groups.

Checkpoint

In this investigation, you saw how a matrix can be used to represent and help analyze a graph.

a A matrix corresponding to a graph that has five vertices, *A, B, C, D,* and *E,* in that order, has a 2 in the third row, fifth column. What does the 2 represent? What does a 1 in the first row, second column mean?

b Explain the differences between the row sums of matrices for graphs with and without Euler circuits. Explain the differences between the row sums for graphs with and without Euler paths.

Be prepared to share your thinking with the entire class.

Think About This Situation

Seven new radio stations are planning to start broadcasting in the same region of the country. The FCC wants to assign a frequency to each station so that no two stations interfere with each other. The FCC also wants to assign the fewest possible number of new frequencies.

a What factors need to be considered before the frequencies can be assigned?

b What method can the FCC use to assign the frequencies?

Radio Station Problem

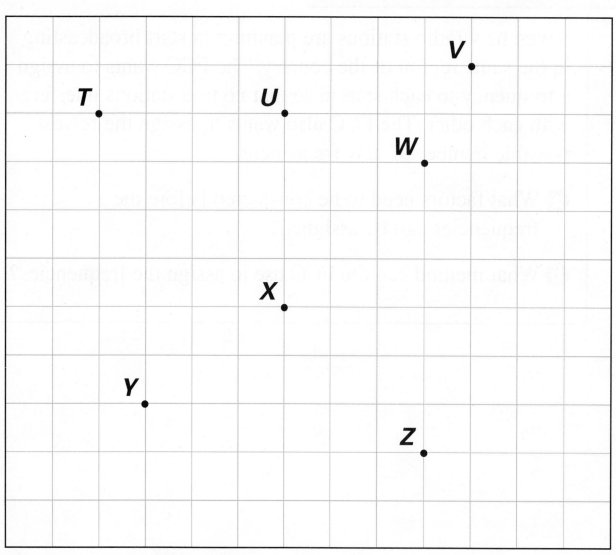

Scale: ⊢——⊣ = **100 miles**

Radio Station Coloring

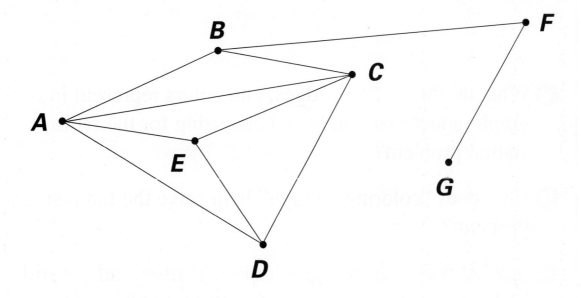

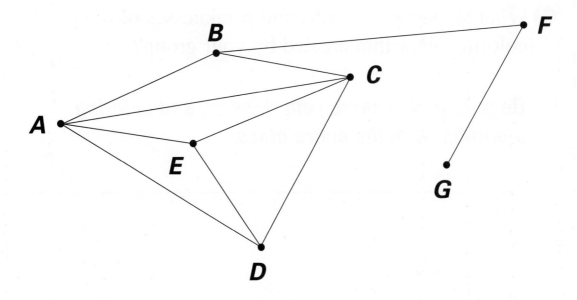

Checkpoint

a What do the vertices, edges, and colors represent in the graph model that you have been using for the radio station problem?

b How does "coloring a graph" help solve the radio station problem?

c In what ways can two graph models differ and yet still both accurately represent a given situation?

d What are some strengths and weaknesses of the graph-coloring algorithm created by your group?

Be prepared to share your thinking and coloring algorithm with the entire class.

Southern Africa, 1980

Map Coloring

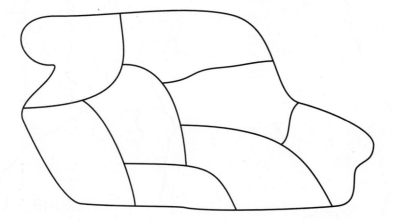

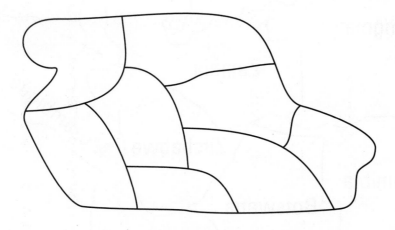

Checkpoint

In this lesson, you have seen three different problems that can be modeled by graph coloring:

■ assigning frequencies to radio stations

■ scheduling club meetings

■ coloring maps

The title of this lesson is "Managing Conflicts." Explain how graph coloring allows you to "manage conflicts" in each of the three problems.

Be prepared to share your explanations with the entire class.

South America

MASTER 109

Sierpinski Triangle

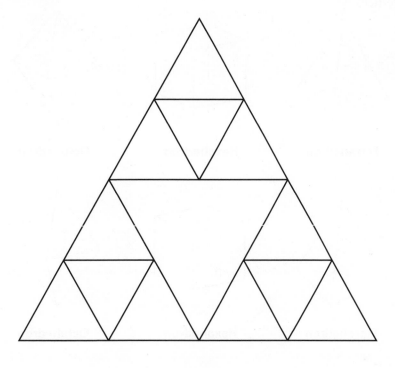

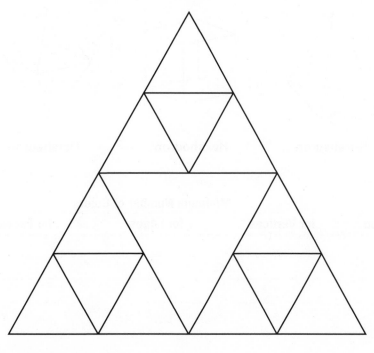

Use with page 288.

**MASTER
110**

Coloring Polyhedra

a. Color the vertices.

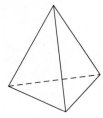   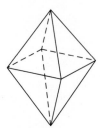   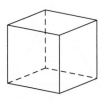

Tetrahedron   **Hexahedron**   **Octahedron**

b. Color the edges.

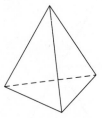   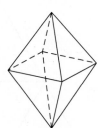   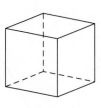

Tetrahedron   **Hexahedron**   **Octahedron**

c. Color the faces.

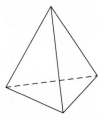   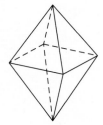   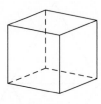

Tetrahedron   **Hexahedron**   **Octahedron**

	Minimum Number of Colors		
Regular Polyhedron	**for Vertices**	**for Edges**	**for Faces**
Tetrahedron			
Hexahedron			
Octahedron			

Sierpinski Triangle

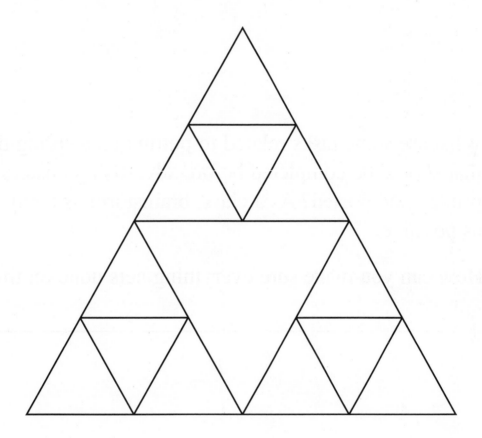

Think About This Situation

a What are some tasks related to putting on a spring dance that should be completed before advertising posters are printed and posted? As a class, brainstorm as many tasks as possible.

b How can you make sure everything gets done on time?

Checkpoint

The digraph showing how tasks involved in the dance project are related to each other is a mathematical model of the situation.

ⓐ What do the vertices of the project digraph represent?

ⓑ How are tasks that can be worked on at the same time represented in the project digraph?

ⓒ How are prerequisite tasks represented in the project digraph?

Be prepared to discuss your digraph and compare it to those of other groups.

Checkpoint

ⓐ How can you find the EFT by examining a digraph for a project?

ⓑ Why is the critical path for a project "critical"?

Be prepared to share your thinking with the entire class.

Scheduling a Project

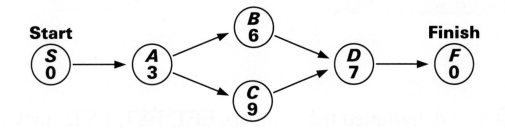

Task	EST	LST	EFT	Slack Time	Critical Task?
A	____	____	____	_____	_____
B	____	____	____	_____	_____
C	____	____	____	_____	_____
D	____	____	____	_____	_____

Checkpoint

a You determined the numbers EFT, EST, LST, slack time, and scheduled time to begin. Summarize what these numbers mean and how they are related to each other.

b How can you use the digraph for a given project and the numbers EFT, EST, LST, slack time, and scheduled time to begin, to make sure that the project gets done on time?

Be prepared to share your management ideas with the entire class.

Checkpoint

a What are some possible methods for planning a project when the exact times for finishing certain tasks are not known?

b Which method do you think is the best? Why?

Be prepared to share your thinking with the entire class.

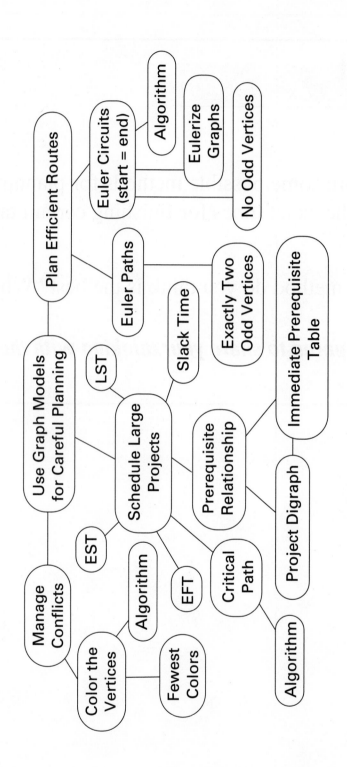

First Floor Offices

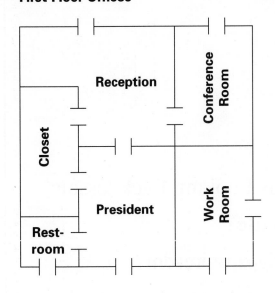

Second Floor Offices

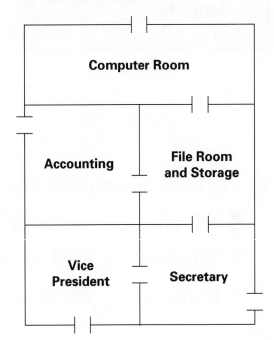

Checkpoint

a For each of the problems in this Looking Back lesson:

- Which graph model did you use?

- What did the vertices and edges represent?

- Explain why you chose the graph model you used.

b For each of the graph models you have studied—Euler circuits and paths, graph coloring, and critical paths— describe the types of problems that can be solved using the model.

Be prepared to share your descriptions and explanations with the entire class.

Constructing a Math Toolkit
Concepts/Definitions/Relationships and Properties

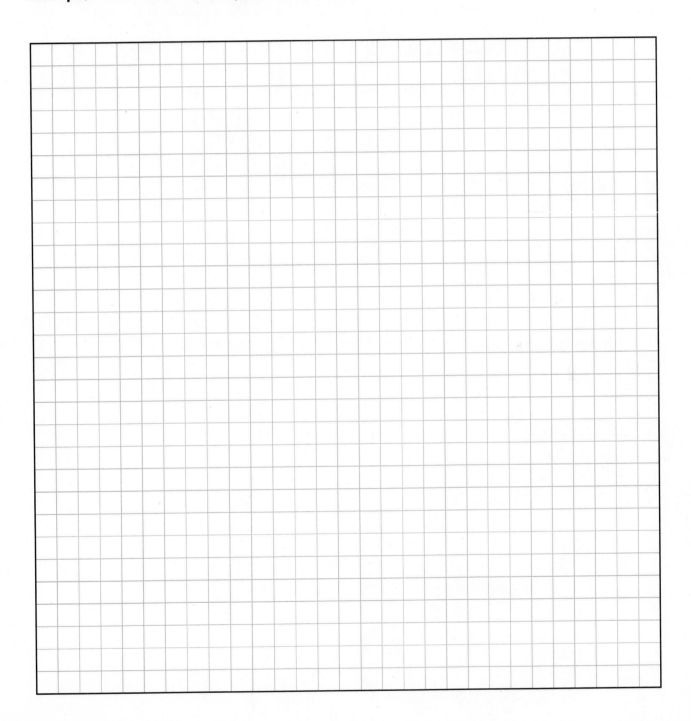

Constructing a Math Toolkit
Concepts/Definitions/Relationships and Properties

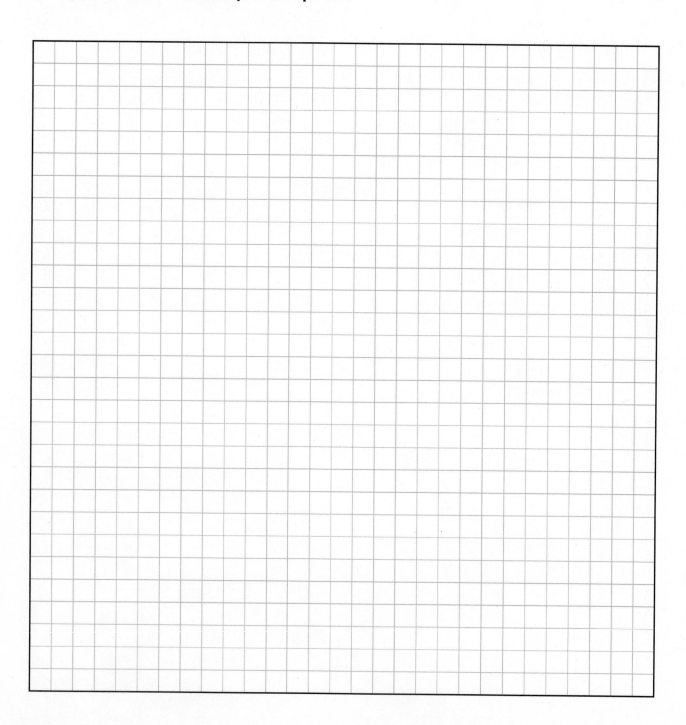

Constructing a Math Toolkit
Concepts/Definitions/Relationships and Properties

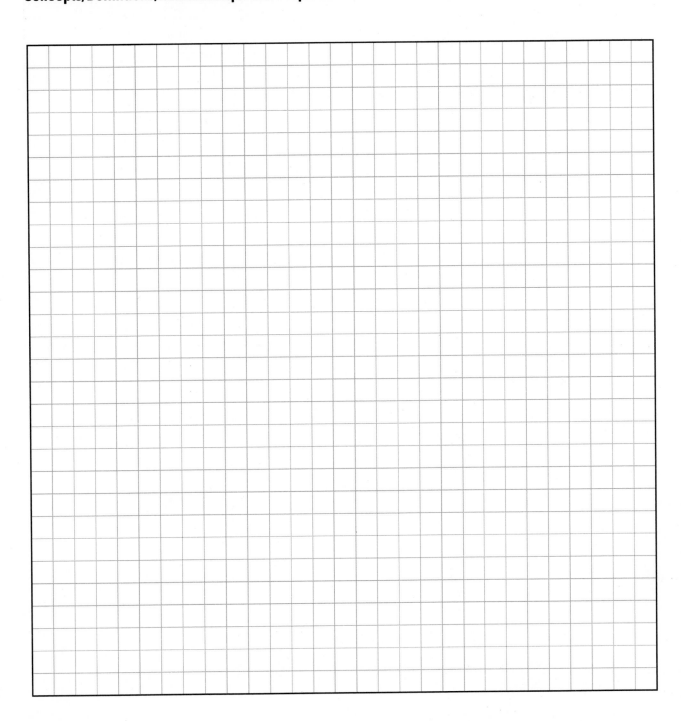

Constructing a Math Toolkit
Concepts/Definitions/Relationships and Properties

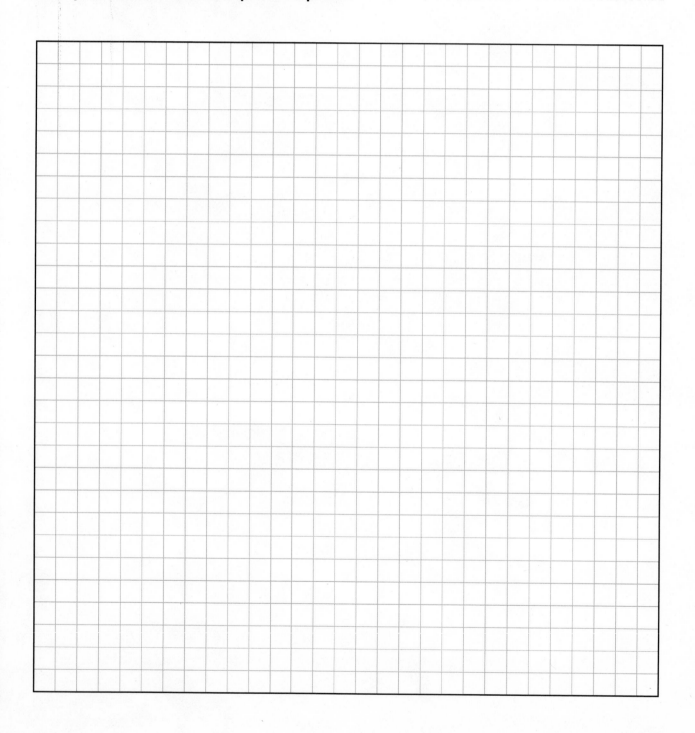

Constructing a Math Toolkit

Group Work

1. Discuss and decide responses to Activities _____ on page(s) _____. Each group member must help to give ideas and opinions.

2. Random reporters will be selected for class discussion.

3. Questions will be accepted from groups only, and any member of the group may be called upon to ask the question.

   You have _____ min. to work

   (from _____:_____ to _____:_____).

Evaluating My Group Work

	Yes	Somewhat	No
1. I participated in this investigation by contributing ideas.	_____	_____	_____
2. I was considerate of others, showed appreciation of ideas, and encouraged others to respond.	_____	_____	_____
3. I paraphrased others' responses and asked others to explain their thinking and work.	_____	_____	_____
4. I listened carefully and disagreed in an agreeable manner.	_____	_____	_____
5. I checked others' understanding of the work.	_____	_____	_____
6. I helped others in the group understand the solution(s) and strategies.	_____	_____	_____
7. We all agreed on the solution(s).	_____	_____	_____
8. I stayed on task and got the group back to work when necessary.	_____	_____	_____
9. We asked the teacher for assistance only if everyone in the group had the same question.	_____	_____	_____

10. What actions helped the group work productively?

11. What actions could make the group even more productive tomorrow?

Your signature: _____

Plots

——— , page ———

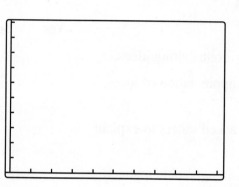

——— , page ———

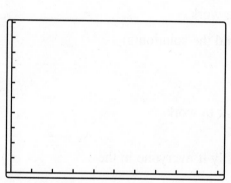

——— , page ———

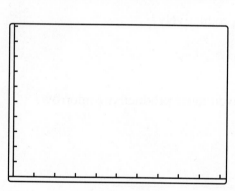

——— , page ———

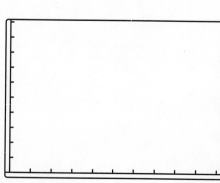

Graphs

_____, page _____

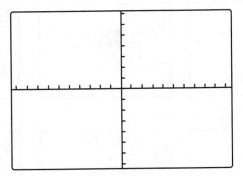

```
WINDOW
 Xmin= _____
 Xmax= _____
 Xscl= _____
 Ymin= _____
 Ymax= _____
 Yscl= _____
```

_____, page _____

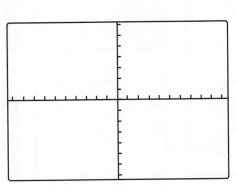

```
WINDOW
 Xmin= _____
 Xmax= _____
 Xscl= _____
 Ymin= _____
 Ymax= _____
 Yscl= _____
```

_____, page _____

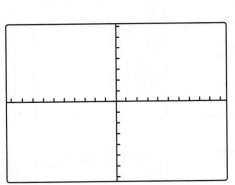

```
WINDOW
 Xmin= _____
 Xmax= _____
 Xscl= _____
 Ymin= _____
 Ymax= _____
 Yscl= _____
```

_____, page _____

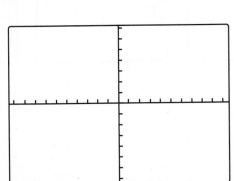

```
WINDOW
 Xmin= _____
 Xmax= _____
 Xscl= _____
 Ymin= _____
 Ymax= _____
 Yscl= _____
```

Y=

```
Y1=
Y2=
Y3=
Y4=
Y5=
Y6=
Y7=
Y8=
```

STAT PLOT (2nd Y=)

```
STAT PLOTS
1 Plot1...
   Off ⤶ L1 L2 □
2: Plot2...
   Off ⤶ L1 L3 +
3: Plot3...
   Off ⤶ L1 L4 .
4↓PlotsOff
```

PLOT 1

```
Plot1
On Off
Type: ▣ ⤶ ▥ ▥
Xlist: L1 L2 L3 L4 L5 L6
Ylist: L1 L2 L3 L4 L5 L6
Mark: □ + .
```

WINDOW

```
WINDOW FORMAT
Xmin=-10
Xmax=10
Xscl=1
Ymin=-10
Ymax=10
Yscl=1
```

WINDOW FORMAT

```
WINDOW FORMAT
RectGC  PolarGC
CoordOn  CoordOff
GridOff  GridOn
AxesOn  AxesOff
LabelOff  LabelOn
```

TBLSET (2nd WINDOW)

```
TABLE SETUP
 TblMin=1
 △Tbl=1
Indpnt: Auto Ask
Depend: Auto Ask
```

ZOOM

```
ZOOM MEMORY
1 ZBox
2: Zoom In
3: Zoom Out
4: ZDecimal
5: ZSquare
6: ZStandard
7↓ZTrig
```

ZOOM

```
ZOOM MEMORY
3↑Zoom Out
4: ZDecimal
5: ZSquare
6: ZStandard
7: ZTrig
8: ZInteger
9 ZoomStat
```

CALC (2nd TRACE)

```
CALCULATE
1 value
2: root
3: minimum
4: maximum
5: intersect
6: dy/dx
7: ∫f(x)dx
```

MODE

```
Normal Sci Eng
Float 0123456789
Radian Degree
Func Par Pol Seq
Connected Dot
Sequential Simul
FullScreen Split
```

LINK (2nd X,T,θ)

```
SEND RECEIVE
1 SelectAll+...
2: SelectAll-...
3: SelectCurrent...
4: Back Up...
```

RECEIVE

```
SEND RECEIVE
1 Receive
```

STAT

```
EDIT CALC
1 Edit...
2: SortA(
3: SortD(
4: ClrList
```

STAT CALC

```
EDIT CALC
1 1-Var Stats
2: 2-Var Stats
3: SetUp...
4: Med-Med
5: LinReg(ax+b)
6: QuadReg
7↓CubicReg
```

LIST OPS (2nd STAT)

```
OPS MATH
1 SortA(
2: SortD(
3: dim
4: Fill(
5: seq(
```

LIST MATH (2nd STAT)

```
OPS MATH
1 min(
2: max(
3: mean(
4: median(
5: sum
6: prod
```

MATH

```
MATH NUM HYP PRB
1 ▶Frac
2: ▶Dec
3: ³
4: ³√
5: ˣ√
6: fMin(
7↓fMax(
```

MATH NUM

```
MATH NUM HYP PRB
1 round(
2: iPart
3: fPart
4: int
5: min(
6: max(
```

MATH PRB

```
MATH NUM HYP PRB
1 rand
2: nPr
3: nCr
4: !
```

VARS

```
VARS
1 Window...
2: Zoom...
3: GDB...
4: Picture...
5: Statistics...
6: Table...
```

Y-VARS (2nd MATH)

```
Y-VARS
1 Function...
2: Parametric...
3: Polar...
4: Sequence...
5: On/Off...
```

Y=
```
Plot1 Plot2 Plot3
\Y₁=
\Y₂=
\Y₃=
\Y₄=
\Y₅=
\Y₆=
\Y₇=
```

STAT PLOT (2nd Y=)
```
STAT PLOTS
1:Plot1…Off
   L1    1
2:Plot2…Off
   L1    L3    +
3:Plot3…Off
   L1    L2    □
4↓PlotsOff
```

PLOT 1
```
Plot1 Plot2 Plot3
On Off
Type: ⌐ ⌐ ⊞
Xlist:L1
Ylist:L3
Mark: □ + ·
```

WINDOW
```
WINDOW
Xmin=-10
Xmax=10
Xscl=1
Ymin=-10
Ymax=10
Yscl=1
Xres=1
```

TBLSET (2nd WINDOW)
```
TABLE SETUP
 TblStart=1
 △Tbl=1
Indpnt: Auto Ask
Depend: Auto Ask
```

ZOOM
```
ZOOM MEMORY
1:ZBox
2:Zoom In
3:Zoom Out
4:ZDecimal
5:ZSquare
6:ZStandard
7↓ZTrig
```

ZOOM
```
ZOOM MEMORY
4↑ZDecimal
5:ZSquare
6:ZStandard
7:ZTrig
8:ZInteger
9:ZoomStat
0:ZoomFit
```

CALC (2nd TRACE)
```
CALCULATE
1:value
2:zero
3:minimum
4:maximum
5:intersect
6:dy/dx
7:∫f(x)dx
```

FORMAT (2nd ZOOM)
```
RectGC PolarGC
CoordOn CoordOff
GridOff GridOn
AxesOn AxesOff
LabelOff LabelOn
ExprOn ExprOff
```

MODE
```
Normal Sci Eng
Float 0123456789
Radian Degree
Func Par Pol Seq
Connected Dot
Sequential Simul
Real a+bi re^θi
Full Horiz G-T
```

LINK (2nd X,T,θ,n)
```
SEND RECEIVE
1:All+…
2:All-…
3:Prgm…
4:List…
5:Lists to TI82…
6:GDB…
7↓Pic…
```

RECEIVE
```
SEND RECEIVE
1:Receive
```

STAT
```
EDIT CALC TESTS
1:Edit…
2:SortA(
3:SortD(
4:ClrList
5:SetUpEditor
```

STAT CALC
```
EDIT CALC TESTS
1:1-Var Stats
2:2-Var Stats
3:Med-Med
4:LinReg(ax+b)
5:QuadReg
6:CubicReg
7↓QuartReg
```

LIST OPS (2nd STAT)
```
NAMES OPS MATH
1:SortA(
2:SortD(
3:dim(
4:Fill(
5:seq(
6:cumSum(
7↓△List(
```

LIST MATH (2nd STAT)
```
NAMES OPS MATH
1:min(
2:max(
3:mean(
4:median(
5:sum(
6:prod(
7↓stdDev(
```

MATH
```
MATH NUM CPX PRB
1:▶Frac
2:▶Dec
3:³
4:³√(
5:ˣ√
6:fMin(
7↓fMax(
```

MATH NUM
```
MATH NUM CPX PRB
1:abs(
2:round(
3:iPart(
4:fPart(
5:int(
6:min(
7↓max(
```

MATH PRB
```
MATH NUM CPX PRB
1:rand
2:nPr
3:nCr
4:!
5:randInt(
6:randNorm(
7:randBin(
```

VARS
```
VARS Y-VARS
1:Window…
2:Zoom…
3:GDB…
4:Picture…
5:Statistics…
6:Table…
7:String…
```

VARS Y-VARS
```
VARS Y-VARS
1:Function…
2:Parametric…
3:Polar…
4:On/Off…
```

© Glencoe/McGraw-Hill

Square Dot Paper

Isometric Dot Paper

UNIT 1

Patterns in Data

In the "Patterns in Data" unit, you used graphical displays of distributions to uncover important patterns in data. You also used measures of center and variation to help you summarize and interpret specific aspects of the data.

When describing the overall pattern in a set of data, what features should you look for and include in your description?

_____

_____

_____

_____

In this unit, you learned how to make several different kinds of plots. Each plot is useful in different situations and with different types of data. For each type of plot below, describe how to create it, what information you can get by examining it, and when it might be useful.

Stem-and-leaf plot _____

_____

_____

Number line plot _____

_____

_____

Histogram _____

_____

_____

Box plot _____

_____

_____

Scatterplot _____

_____

_____

Plot over time _____

_____

_____

When summarizing data, you used both measures of center and measures of variation. Describe how to find each of the following statistics and what it tells you about a set of data.

Mean _____

_____

_____

Median _____

_____

_____

Mode _____

_____

_____

Range _____

_____

_____

Interquartile range _____

_____

_____

Mean absolute deviation _____

_____

_____

Some of the above statistics are resistant to outliers and others are not. Describe what it means to be resistant to outliers and identify how each of the above statistics is affected by the presence of outliers in a data set.

_____

_____

_____

_____

UNIT
1

Transforming a set of data by adding a constant to each value or multiplying each value by a positive constant affects measures of center and measures of variation in predictable ways. For each summary statistic on the previous sheet, describe the effect of:

■ Adding a constant a to each value in a data set _____

_____

_____

■ Multiplying each value by a positive constant b _____

_____

_____

UNIT 2

Patterns of Change

In the "Patterns of Change" unit, you explored how to use algebraic ideas to describe and analyze relations between quantitative variables. You used scatterplots to display data and then investigated how graphs and equations can be used to model the patterns in those plots. You also used the models you found to help you answer questions about the situations.

Explain what a *variable* is and what it means to say that one variable *is a function of* another variable or that one variable *depends on* another.

_____

_____

_____

_____

Identify some common pairs of related variables that appear in problem situations. For each example, draw a sketch showing how change in one variable relates to change in the other.

_____   _____

_____   _____

_____   _____

_____   _____

UNIT
2

You used tables, graphs, and equations to model relations between variables.

■ Describe the characteristics of relations between variables that can be modeled well by *NOW-NEXT* equations.

_____

_____

_____

■ Explain what equations like $NEXT = NOW + 5.25$ or $NEXT = 1.25NOW - 50$ tell in such cases.

_____

_____

_____

■ Explain what information about a relationship is provided by equations like $y = 5 + 10x$ or $y = -16t^2 + 4$.

_____

_____

_____

Explain how equations in the "$y = ...$" form can be used to produce graphs and numeric tables illustrating relations.

_____

_____

_____

_____

Describe how you can use a calculator or computer software to produce tables and graphs of relations between variables.

_____

_____

_____

_____

Explain how tables and graphs of relations can be used to help answer questions about those relations.

_____

_____

_____

_____

UNIT 3

Linear Models

In the "Linear Models" unit, you learned how to recognize and interpret linear relationships: one of the most important families of relations between variables. You learned how to model linear relations with graphs, tables of values, and symbolic rules. You then wrote and solved equations and inequalities to answer questions about situations. You also learned how to find the rate of change and explained what it told you about the relationship.

Describe the types of situations that can be modeled well by linear relationships.

_____

_____

_____

_____

Describe the patterns in data tables and plots that indicate a linear relation between variables.

_____

_____

_____

_____

You used two different forms of equations to model linear relations. Describe how to write linear equations in *NOW-NEXT* form and in "$y = ...$" form given

■ a table of values

_____

_____

■ a graph

_____

_____

■ a description of the problem.

_____

_____

Name Date

UNIT 3

Unit Summary

For each equation, explain what a and b tell you about the relationship being modeled.

- $NEXT = NOW + b$, starting at a

- $y = a + bx$

Given a linear graph, explain how you can find each of the following and then describe what each tells you about the relation between the variables expressed in the graph.

- slope

- x-intercept

- y-intercept

Explain how you can determine the slope, x-intercept, and y-intercept if you are given an equation model for the relation.

Describe the relationships between the graphs of $y = 3x + 5$, $y = -3x + 5$, and $y = 3x$.

_____

_____

_____

_____

Describe how you can solve equations like $4.5x + 12.2 = 34.7$ or $4.5x + 12.2 = -24 + 18.2x$ using:

■ tables of values

_____

_____

■ graphs

_____

_____

■ symbolic reasoning

_____

_____

Describe how you can solve inequalities like $4.5x + 12.2 \le 34.7$ or $4.5x + 12.2 > -24 + 18.2x$.

_____

_____

_____

_____

Explain how you can determine if two algebraic expressions are equivalent.

_____

_____

_____

_____

Graph Models

In the "Graph Models" unit, you have seen how vertex-edge graphs can be used to represent and analyze relationships in many contexts. You learned to use three types of graph models.

Complete the following table.

Graph Model	Description	Sample Applications (at least 2 each)
Euler Paths		
Critical Paths		
Vertex Coloring		

Now look more closely at the tools and techniques that you have learned in this unit.

Describe criteria for determining whether a graph has an Euler circuit by inspecting the graph and by inspecting the adjacency matrix that represents the graph.

_____

_____

_____

Repeat the previous task for an Euler path that is not an Euler circuit.

_____

_____

_____

Describe an algorithm for finding an Euler path for a connected graph. Give an example of a graph in which you apply your algorithm.

_____

_____

_____

Of a dozen kinds of fish, some can be put in the same tank and others cannot. Explain how graph coloring might be used to "manage conflicts" in this situation.

_____

_____

_____

_____

Summarize the meanings of the numbers EFT, EST, LST, slack time, and scheduled time to begin when scheduling a large project.

_____

_____

_____

_____

_____

Explain how you can use the digraph for a large project and the above numbers to make sure that the project gets done on time.

_____

_____

_____

_____

_____

_____